Praise for *Fail More*

Fail More, a seemingly paradoxical title, is actually a diagram for winning in work, relationships, and life. Through fascinating stories and examples—as well as concrete tools—this book is a life-changer! No one makes it to the top without having failed. Wooditch is "on point" again!

—**PAUL NEMIROFF, PHD, MD, FACS**
NATIONALLY RECOGNIZED SURGEON AND AUTHOR OF
NINE LIVES: A STORY OF SURVIVAL AND HOPE: OVERCOMING
OBSTACLES, LABELS, AND BEATING THE ODDS

Understanding how to succeed comes from a heavy dose of failing and being resilient. Bill explains in this engaging book how failing teaches us more lessons than succeeding. *Fail More* reveals a great map of clarity on how failure can become our friend and mentor.

—**LEONARD WHEELER**
8 YEAR NFL VETERAN, NFL EXECUTIVE DIRECTOR,
NASCAR PERFORMANCE COACH, AUTHOR, AND SPEAKER

Bill Wooditch nails it! Through revealing personal anecdotes and citing the examples of others, he shows how failure is not only part of everybody's journey to success, but an outcome we need to embrace if we're ever going to achieve greatness. This book is the way forward!

—**SCOTT BURROWS**
MOTIVATIONAL KEYNOTE SPEAKER AND
BESTSELLING AUTHOR OF *VISION MINDSET GRIT*

FAIL MORE

EMBRACE, LEARN, AND ADAPT TO FAILURE AS A WAY TO SUCCESS

BILL WOODITCH

NEW YORK CHICAGO SAN FRANCISCO
ATHENS LONDON MADRID
MEXICO CITY MILAN NEW DELHI
SINGAPORE SYDNEY TORONTO

1 2 3 4 5 6 7 8 9   QVS   24 23 22 21 20 19

ISBN   978-1-260-44151-2
MHID   1-260-44151-2

eISBN   978-1-260-44152-9
eMHID   1-260-44152-0

McGraw-Hill Education books are available at special quantity discounts to use as premiums and sales promotions or for use in corporate training programs. To contact a representative, please visit the Contact Us pages at www.mhprofessional.com.

This book is dedicated to the memory of Curt Brown, Sr.

Client, mentor, and friend—your passion for work
was only exceeded by your love of deep sea fishing.
Not a day goes by that I don't feel the deepest appreciation
for the man you helped me become.

Acknowledgments

To Kelsey McDaniel, the *sine qua non* of this book. You helped me refine my raw voice while keeping this rambling, discursive writer on point. Your unwillingness to cede or compromise quality on the altar of expedience made me and by association, this book, better. I couldn't ask for a more prepared, professional and creative partner.

To my publisher, McGraw Hill, who kept me on tight deadlines and was unwavering in the pursuit of excellence.

To Steve Carlis, who tirelessly worked with me for months on a subject I never would've broached without him.

And to Angela, who opened my heart to possibilities that have now become reality—you lifted me from the fog of frustration and inspired me to push forward.

Contents

Introduction

There are no secrets to success.
It is the result of preparation,
hard work, and learning from failure.
—COLIN POWELL

If you want to be successful, you need to fail more!

I can write fancy motivation to try to trick you into thinking you can avoid failure, or I can just tell you my truth—either you need to do something and you do it, or you don't want something bad enough and you don't do it. The common thread that connects every successful person you'll read about in this book is that they all found failure to be essential and instructive in their pursuit of greatness. Failure was part of their recipe for success.

It's a fact that everything you do involves an element of risk and failure; the only thing that varies is the degree and nature. Wise choices inspire growth, engender happiness, and imbue you with the confidence needed to push the risk envelope further. Poor choices sap your confidence, result in worst-case consequences, and force you to lament the risk you took.

This book will not only identify your failures; it will dissect them, poking and prodding to see what went wrong and why. We will look closely at the anatomy of a fail. We will then talk about how to learn from your mistakes and missteps and—most importantly—how to apply them in your next endeavor. You can't let failure stop you from trying again. A failure only stops you if you don't get back up. In order to overcome that first hurdle, however, we have to put failure on the sidelines for a moment and dive into fear.

Your innate fears as an infant were the fear of falling and the fear of loud noises. After that, your fears came as a result of exposure to life. These fears may have come from experiences at the playground, in the classroom, or even at the family dinner table. Maybe you were called on to read something out loud in class and you mispronounced a word. The shame you feel is something you never want to experience again. This shame only gets heavier each time you resist exposure to those things that could draw attention, judgment, and ridicule. Now don't recoil—it's the very things that make you uncomfortable that you must expose yourself to, to bring you a familiarity and confidence.

About *Fail More*

Fail More isn't a license to intentionally flunk life one mistake at a time. Rather, the focus of this book is on improvement—continual improvement through intentional practice, the willingness to embrace the process, and the ability to learn from the result. Success and failure *both* leave room for improvement. Inside every success there are remnants of failure, and in every failure there are pockets of success. Sustained success is the product of preparation, hard work, and the willingness to learn from the lessons of failure. It is only through trying more that you can become more, learn more, and enjoy more. Dissecting and applying the lessons of your failure is part of preparing for success. You can't have one without the other.

I know risk is a scary word, but risk is also a part of life and will have already become the product of your choices. The choices you make today will dictate your standard of life in the future. From time to time, you may make a bad choice, but the willingness to learn and apply the lesson from these choices will influence your chances of future success.

Experience is the residue of failure. You must learn from the lessons of failure; otherwise it's just an experience. The only way out of a bad situation is through choice—one that is made when you learn from the past. The past can be a learning forum for those mistakes you made, and through the pages of this book, we will learn how to apply the lessons to improve your life.

. . . .

Fail More also doesn't mean you should flub up your product intentionally. Instead, failing more happens when you do mess up and find a way to correct the mistake through the skills you adopt and lessons you learn.

The book will help you view failure as an unconditional requirement for success. This book will give you the tools to move through failure on your journey to success. This book will help you to better understand the nature of your fears and the reasons why you fear failure. It will also provide you with ways to navigate rejection, fear, and failure. Ultimately, it will be up to you to do the tough work and apply what you've learned. If you want to improve, you will. If you don't, you won't. If you are determined to improve, you'll embrace, as fact, the concept that failure is now no longer an excuse; it's an asset. When people fear, they stop finding ways to thrive and start thinking of ways to survive.

I've realized long ago that perfect is the enemy of good. I've also come to accept the idea that in life, the most you can ever become is good. Perfect isn't part of the human condition. We all need to back off, hit the brakes, and give ourselves permission to screw things up once in a while.

. . . .

I wrote this book to give you the information you need to understand failure from an unemotional perspective and grow from it. When you can gain this perspective, you will begin to view failure as an experiment, or a series of trials and possible errors that bring you closer to your goal. The iron law of success is that nothing worthy of your time and effort can happen without your willingness to face fear and learn from the lessons of your failures.

Learning from Failure Will
Change the Dynamic of Your Life

Think of "failing more" as "trying more." It's a strategic way to collect and apply tactical knowledge and methods you can use for future benefit. *Fail More* isn't a license to engage in irresponsible behavior—the type that causes physical harm or turns you into the class clown. Instead, *Fail More* will teach you to learn from the lessons of failure. It's a road map to succeeding, a rational way to achieve in spite of the fears and failures that we all encounter.

You will wage battle against the need for certainty and the discomfort of uncertainty. Leaning into the discomfort of uncertainty is the path to growth. When you step into uncertainty, you expose yourself to the new, which is often the difficult, yet always the most vital choice you'll make toward personal betterment.

When you seek out uncertainty, you are opening your mind to possibility. You're a student of life, inquiring and seeking ways and means to illuminate your quest for success. You're open to what you might find. Does this mean you have to accept all that you discover? No, you can reject what doesn't feel right. But you do have to stay inquisitive. You need to be the creator and the innovator, always in search of new ideas or methods that create value. Don't leave behind the lessons you learned from past failures. You will need them to successfully take that next step.

Chapter Summaries:
Your Blueprint for Success

Each chapter of this book has been developed with interconnected lessons and methods designed to help you learn from *failure* on your quest for success. An overview is provided for your efficient use of this book as a manual for success. My express intent is to allow you to look back at chapters that can provide takeaways and teachable components that you can apply for use *now*.

Chapter 1: Always Forward:
Achievement Is on the Other Side of Failure

Success is a process that is always under construction. In this chapter, I'll blast back to my past, when the only prescription I had for success was on a 6-inch ruler. That ruler, through its etched inscription, revealed what would be for me the way forward to success. In this chapter, I will challenge you to seek out failure. Now you may never welcome, embrace, or befriend failure, but if you demand success, failure is never going away. Failure is an indispensable teacher if you are a serious student of success.

You'll also meet the billionaire who couldn't get a job at KFC. You'll learn how to stifle that negative voice that says, "You can't, you won't, and you shouldn't." And you'll learn what to do when failure inevitably shows up to derail your progress. Dissecting and learning from failure led to massive success for so many; I want you to learn from their experiences in addition to your own.

Chapter 2: The Greats Have Learned
the Art of *Failing More*

What do "the greats" have in common? Each has failed countless times before basking in the bright lights of success. They have learned that failing more is the way to success. In this chapter, you'll learn from some of the most successful and brilliant people in the world and understand that they treat their life as a series of innovations where trial and error go hand in hand with achievement and success.

Chapter 3: Recognize Fear

We're going to dissect the source of fear and gain the knowledge you need to rationally examine your personal fears. You will learn the difference between fear and danger and be able to use this information every day, whether you're navigating traffic or negotiating a million-dollar proposal.

Chapter 4: Break Through the
Obstacles That Limit Success

Learning to move through fear and navigate obstacles that impede your progress is crucial to your development. The first and perhaps most formidable obstacle you need to overcome is the fear of making an attempt in the first place.

This book won't just help you analyze failures; it will also help you inspect your fears. In this chapter, you'll learn how to take your fears apart and dissect them rationally instead of reacting to them emotionally. You will learn that to fail more is to gain more control over fear. We'll start with the small steps, and your confidence and competence will grow each time you lean into the uncomfortable. Once you master the familiar, you'll be ready for the next challenge where the pain of discomfort will await you once again. Get used to the discomfort. It's the price of progress!

Chapter 5: Become a Master of Failure

Here we get into the nuts and bolts of dissecting past failures. In this chapter, you'll meet Carol Dweck, the Stanford researcher who coined the terms "fixed mindset" and "growth mindset." You'll learn which of these mindsets can help you adapt to failure and which one is a detriment to your progress.

You'll also learn how to create an objective framework to evaluate failure from a logical perspective, avoid the pattern of failure, and move from an emotional response to a logical action. Each specific failure will provide you with an opportunity to improve by giving you clues how not to fail.

Chapter 6: It's Goal Time: Define and Plan for Success

Many people work with "fuzzy" ideas and create incomplete goals that result in a distorted view of accomplishment. We will look at why failure may have occurred and the planning that could have prevented it. This chapter will show you the importance of establishing clear goals and teach you exactly how to set effective goals for yourself. You'll also learn how to establish subgoals to fail your way forward toward your big goal and create momentum.

Chapter 7: The Road to Success

Success is a journey, not a destination. You can't park it in hopes that it will flourish in a vacuum of inattention and inactivity.

In this chapter, you'll learn how to narrow your options in a competing universe of distractions. What sorts of distractions have hindered you in the past? We will look at what they are and how they got in your way. Too many options can become one major distraction, so I'll teach you how to stay focused on the one thing you can master, that's most important to your success.

Chapter 8: Embrace Risk

First, before you embrace risk, you'll learn the questions you need to ask to limit your exposure to failure. You'll learn about trade-offs and the importance of knowing what you want before you even think about taking a risk. This chapter will arm you with a weapon that will lessen the severity of fear and teach you a mental trick that can make risk and fear less daunting.

Chapter 9: Success Is a Process,
Not a Destination

Life serves adversity as a barrier to entry in the pursuit of happiness. Seek to learn what it takes to turn adversity into an advantage.

In this chapter, you will learn the true measure of success. Your journey to success will introduce you to Steve Harvey, David Neeleman, and J.K. Rowling, three people who dealt with tremendous failure and, in time, learned to use its teaching to become the uber-successful people they are today.

Chapter 10: Maintain a Mindset for Continued Success

Stagnation is a success killer. Stagnation comes from a little too much comfort and avoidance of the things you have to do to keep success flowing forward. Stagnation is a fixed mindset that defines success as the product of innate ability. When met with an insoluble problem, people with this mindset quit, and they're not just quitting on the problem; they're quitting on life. I will show you why the power is in the struggle and how to avoid this debilitating condition that is stagnation.

Fail More Takeaways

At the end of each chapter, you will see takeaways titled "Framing Failure." These are the steps required to master each chapter's challenge. For our purposes, framing is defined as "making a construct by fitting parts together or in accordance with a plan." Our takeaways are designed with the following plan in mind: Use the takeaways today to start making changes in your life now. They're exportable and fully developed for immediate use.

CHAPTER 1

Always Forward
Achievement Is on the Other Side of Failure

A little more persistence, a little more effort, and what seemed hopeless failure may turn to glorious success."

—ELBERT HUBBARD

Would You Bankroll Yourself?

M y first memorable encounter with failure was doled out, face down on my desk, courtesy of my eighth-grade algebra teacher. For 60 minutes each day, I struggled through that class. I was assigned to the second seat, first row from the door.

I would bring my algebra book home, open it, look at it, then close it. It bore no marks of use, not one highlight, not one dog-ear. It still had that brand-new book smell at semester's end. The subject was not only uncomfortable for me, but distasteful as well. Instead of struggling through

1

my homework, I would pick up a football, knock on my neighbors' doors, and get a pickup game going in the front yard. It was more fun quarterbacking my ragtag team to the imagined Super Bowl than it was to figure out the quadratic formula.

But the unwillingness to do the uncomfortable comes at a price. This time the price was all-out panic. I watched my teacher begin the slow walk up and down the aisles. Desk by desk, student by student, she handed out the graded tests. "Thank God," I thought, "she's starting on the other side of the room. How fast can I cover my paper up? I think I'll lean forward over my desk and put my hands at the top . . ." I broke out into a sweat. I knew it was coming; I just didn't know how bad. The best I could hope for was a solid D.

Even without the spoken word, you can tell when a person is angry or disappointed. There's a certain reaction, a response that, even in the silence, may reflect disappointment, tension, and condescension. I could feel her presence behind me, and unlike all the other tests, she flipped mine face down and stabbed into it with the sharp nail of her manicured forefinger.

You know the feeling—you think everyone is looking at you, and you want to disappear. I felt that way at that moment. I just knew everyone was trying to guess what was underneath that upside-down sheet. I turned the right edge over and peeked. And there it was: a big, bold, angry mother of an "F"! It was full of anger and condescension in its defiance of my mathematical ability. There were small ink splatters around the flair and bold stroke of that F.

I was overwhelmed by creeping self-doubt. I started to think, "I'll never graduate from high school." It was a hard flunk, judging by the ferocity stamped into that hard-pressed F—an "F you, buddy! You ain't ever getting out of here" flag of failure.

At an early age, our teachers, parents, peers, and the rest of the social order teach us that failure is the result of a lack of innate ability. We're taught to compete for perfection—a zero-sum form of induced combat that pits our genes against the genes of others. Avoidance is our natural inclination, followed by frustration, anger, excuse, and ultimately surrender. We carry the vestiges of this thinking into our businesses and homes. It becomes a part of our life, and we have one of two choices: deal with it and navigate forward in spite of it, or succumb to it and say, "I quit."

A common thread throughout this book is that no person is an island. There isn't one of us who can exist without the help of others. To help me pass the class, my mother hired a tutor. And much to my surprise, even my teacher took an interest in my welfare by helping me after class. I generated enough of a *wobble* that I was able to scrape by with a D, meaning that if you're getting a D, you're not crawling, nor are you walking—you're wobbling.

I didn't know what was happening at the time, but as I sat down to write this book, I reflected on the significance of my first encounter with a type of failure that had real consequences. I thought back to the spectrum of emotions I felt. Embarrassment, ridicule, and self-doubt. I didn't think I was smart enough to pass my math class. The thought turned into a belief that became a self-fulfilling prophecy.

One of the key themes in this book is self-honesty. When I look back, I didn't take the proper steps to overcome this obstacle by accepting my failure as a challenge to improve. In fact, I tried to avoid the subject altogether. If you try to evade the things that are fundamentally important to your growth, you'll pay the price of your neglect at a later date. And when the bill collector knocks on your door, the cost of negligence will eclipse the price you would've paid by facing the fear earlier.

When it came to obstacles that could result in potential failure, I adopted what I call a "cycle of avoidance" that would repeat itself through early adulthood. If it didn't come easily to me, I didn't do it. If I couldn't learn it in a day, it wasn't worth learning. If I thought that trying would result in failure, I started to build excuses: "I'm not ready." "I don't want to do this." "My brain doesn't work that way."

Looking back, I'll never know what opportunities I missed by making those excuses. There's always a reason for a delay. Many people wait for "perfect" before they begin, but perfect isn't just going to show up out of nowhere. We all have to do the gritty and unglamorous work if we're going to push the envelope. You have to put your toes on the edge of "comfortable" and step into the pain of change and cloud of uncertainty to make a real difference in your life. Looking through the rearview mirror at my excuses makes me cringe. Not just because I missed countless opportunities, but also because I left each failure behind me without learning anything from it. I didn't try to look at what I could've done to prevent the failure. I didn't try to grow from failure; I simply discarded that experience behind me and kept walking on the same path.

Breaking the Pattern: The Cycle of Avoidance

Sometimes I engage in useless mental gymnastics by asking myself, "What if?" For example, "What if I would've anchored myself to a desk, handcuffed myself to a book, and spent those hours learning, instead of throwing a football around?" Questions like this are left to the selective narrative you choose to believe. To escape the regret of what-ifs, you must summon the courage to break the cycle of avoidance. When it comes to courage, Franklin D. Roosevelt's words resonate: "Courage is not the absence of fear, but rather the assessment that something else is more important than fear."

And there it is!

The first two steps to failing more productively are to recognize the cycle of avoidance and then have the courage to break the pattern and make the changes vital to growth. This book will teach you how to recognize the origins of your fears. You'll learn where they emanate from and what steps you can take to overcome their limits. Although I will warn you, once you learn the steps through fear and you put them into practice, your forward progress will still be met with obstacles.

Obstacles will only impede your progress, however, if you don't learn how to move through or around them.

You'll learn the importance of making your goals crystal clear. I'll also show you the importance of subgoals, which are incremental steps toward success that make the big goal more realistic.

The road to success isn't easy. If it were, we'd all be wildly successful. Herculean feats aren't required for sustained success. What is required is the persistence and willingness to do something every day that brings you closer to the realization of your dreams. This book is not going to be a simple cheerleader. It is not going to just tell you that all these other people overcame failure and that you can too. It is going to show you that failure doesn't mean your efforts are over. It means they have just begun.

The Poster Boy for Failure

If you want to succeed, you have to fail more. The most significant difference between success and failure is the ability to learn from failure and apply the lessons to create success. Every failure comes with specific teachable moments, each of which deserves your undivided attention. If you don't heed those lessons, your failures are meaningless.

You have your own mental picture of failure, and it's often accompanied by negative feelings. Just thinking of failure can make you grimace and turn away in disgust. It can drive you to a neighbor's with a football under your arm. However, both the picture and feeling are worthy of further study. Failure can be a guide; it's a map that shows you where success lives. Think of life as an experimental lab—you are the innovator of your life, creating concepts that you can test in the field. Some of your ideas work, and some won't, but each trial will give you a little more information, a little more encouragement, and a little more confidence. Each failed attempt will reveal what you have to do to make things work the next time. There can be no success without failure.

Before you look for an inherent contradiction, try to reserve judgment until you learn what real persistence, perseverance, failure, and redemptive success look like. The poster boy for the cover of this book (if I could choose one) would be Jack Ma, a Chinese business magnate, investor, and philanthropist. He found ways to fail that boggle the mind. Soul-crushing, hard-core stuff that would cripple even the strongest and most determined.

Yes, it's true—Churchill, Lincoln, and Einstein failed early and often. Each struggled academically, but they've got nothing on Jack Ma. Failure is relative. It's contingent upon the value you place on the outcome you pursue. For example, after a sanity exam, if I wanted to be the richest man in the world, I would become an utter and complete failure, no matter how many attempts I made. Warren Buffett and Bill Gates aren't moving over for me! Goals have to be realistic and anchored in possibility.

Ma is the first to admit that he wasn't a good student. In fact, he was so deficient that he almost wasn't accepted into middle school. Now that's a rite of passage for most, just by age and stage of life. He recalls: "I failed a key primary school test two times. I failed the middle school test three times. I failed the college entrance exam two times."

7

If it was tough for me to walk into my house with an F once, imagine the feeling Jack Ma had when he walked home countless times with failure in his pocket!

Jack Ma lowers the bar on failure to the subterranean level. He took his college entrance exam and earned a score of less than 1 percent. I think you get more credit here for signing your name on the SATs! It wasn't his failure to prepare that was the problem though; it was his struggles with math. He was as proficient at math as I was, and that level of proficiency looked like a big, red F with splotches around it.

I'll give Ma this—he never lost his aspiration or enthusiasm for success. He applied to and was rejected from Harvard 10 times. Why he applied 10 times is a mystery that to date has been unanswered. When interviewed, Ma said, "The very important thing you should have is patience." File that right next to perseverance, and you've got a snapshot of Jack Ma. But wait, there's more . . .

He applied to be a police officer, but the police wouldn't even give him cursory consideration—prefacing their decision with three words, "You're no good." There were five applicants; Ma was the only one rejected. But all was not lost. KFC was coming to China, and Ma, of course, applied for one of the 23 openings. Of the 24 applicants, only one wasn't hired. Can you guess who that was?

Ma applied and was accepted to Hangzhou Normal University, where he majored in English. After graduation, he applied for 30 different jobs—and failed to land even one of them. Jack knew that math wasn't his thing. Time after time, it was his issues with mathematics that made universities and employers turn him away. He realized that in order to move forward, he was going to have to leave behind the quantitative and focus on the qualitative aspects of his life.

It worked. Ma became fluent in English and secured his first job as an English teacher at the Hangzhou Dianzi University at the age of 24. Ma traveled to the United States in 1995 on an assignment, and he was introduced to the internet. His first search was for "beer." He couldn't find any Chinese entries for beer, so he searched "China" and found no entries for the country either. Never lacking for inspiration, Ma channeled the innovator inside him and thought, "Why don't I make a website related to China?" He partnered with his friend Stuart Trusty, who worked as an internet consultant.

They developed a website, and it did well. But one year later, failure struck again. A state-owned enterprise, Zhejiang Telecom, took over Ma's innovative enterprise. He then moved back to Beijing and assumed a role in the Ministry of Foreign Trade and Economic Cooperation, building websites for the government. Bureaucracy frustrated Ma, and he left to start a new internet venture, Alibaba, which would serve small businesses and would go on to become one of the world's largest companies. In 2018, Jack Ma's net worth was reported to be $40.9 billion, making him the wealthiest man in China. If he hadn't switched his focus to languages, he never would have come to the United States. This one success opened the door to opportunities he never would have had if he just kept applying for the same jobs.

Fail More isn't a license to be irresponsible, or to intentionally flunk life one mistake at a time. Instead, the goal is to constantly improve through intentional practice, while embracing the process and learning from the result. Success and failure both leave room for improvement. It's only through trying more that you can become more, learn more, and enjoy more.

A Foreclosed Future

I was a terrible student in high school. The habits that followed me from my freshman year presaged a future that reflected apathy and, at times, an antipathy toward school. If I opened a book, it was to skim it for pictures.

When my graduating class went off to college, I created my own path. I hung out with the remnants of the "cool crowd." I went to work in a factory, cashed my checks at the local bank, and spent my money at the local watering holes. I didn't save a dime.

Every morning, I would wake up at five o'clock, pull on a wool coat, and put on a yellow hat with the inscription "Miles Ahead" etched on it. Then I began my tired march forward to endure eight hours of boredom.

I punched 3 holes in about 300 pieces of wood that were 18 inches long for 8 hours a day. No deviation; just center the piece of wood and then punch, push, punch, push. I would discard the defective pieces in a pile and keep on fitting, punching, and pushing product.

One day, I got a tap on the shoulder. I was going to get a promotion, a 5 percent hourly raise, and a change in daily activities. The next day, I found myself in the paint room. The paint room was a 12-foot by 12-foot confined space, where I would spend the day spraying veneer over prefab pieces of wood.

As I worked, images morphed into distinct thoughts, painting a bleak picture of my present condition. My present foreshadowed a future that I may have foreclosed through irresponsible choices. It has been my experience that, for most things in life, becoming a victim is a choice (excluding life-threatening or injury-producing events). My thoughts were vivid, accompanied by the pangs of pain and the growing, gnawing angst of my present situation. I felt hopelessness because I knew I was the cause of my own misery. Self-inflicted wounds are the deepest kind of cut. They only heal from the salve of awareness, the resolve to take action, and the corresponding activity that marries need to action.

Now let me make one thing clear. I'm not throwing shade on those who work in a factory. I think that people suited for this work provide for their welfare and the well-being of their family through the toil and physical exercise that is both notable and noble. It's hard work, period. We each have to find our own way in life, locate our gift, and use it. I just felt there was something beyond the boundaries and limits of my upbringing that I personally had to explore. But before I could explore the future, I had to face my biggest fear in the mirror.

All my life, I was told I had potential, in both school and sports, but that statement was followed by the caveat, "But you've got to apply yourself." There it was, peering out from behind the statement: My biggest fear was to actually apply myself, go all in, total immersion. But what if I came up short of my own expectations—would I be a failure?

The key to success is to learn how to progressively adjust and adapt to realize your intended goal or ideal. If you're in sales and you're making calls to generate activity with prospects, you may fail to connect on hundreds of attempts. Then you hit one, two, or three, and through those mini-failures, you're progressing toward the intended result by learning to adjust as you go. As you're applying ice on the bruise of rejection, it may be hard to see the truth that this particular failure is your teacher. If you embrace the lessons, you're answering the bell and getting back in position with the newfound knowledge and hard-won experience that is necessary to keep moving forward.

Your mindset will dictate your reality. Think of failure as a momentary setback, a dress rehearsal for a stage play that will close to a standing ovation. If an actor flubs a line during rehearsal, the producers don't cancel the show. You cannot shut down when faced with failure, no matter how big or small. If you choose to adopt the mindset that success is a process, and failure is an indispensable part of achievement, you're taking the first steps to reframe the negativity associated with failure. When you can reframe it, you can own it, and you can apply your terms to the setback. Know that it comes with a lesson, and apply the teaching.

Expected and Unexpected Ranges of Failure

Any time you try something new, you expose yourself to a threshold of disappointment. Video games are designed for failure. But the thing about video games is that, at least for me, they take my mind off reality. I'm not engaged with my inner dialogue; I'm just focused on the game. There is no confrontational consequence (as there is in life) that makes you think you're failing—you just think you're improving each time you get a little further in the game. I can't tell you how many times I rebooted Madden '18, trying to take my Pittsburgh Steelers to the Super Bowl. I broke a few controllers along the way, but I was able to move from rookie, to veteran, to all pro. Video games are a great analogy for failure. You learn not to take defeat personally. You just reboot and try again. It's process and challenge that you focus on, and you're determined to get the result.

Gaming is in $36 billion industry. Why are video games so popular? As noted above, they are designed for failure. They challenge people. No one wants to download a new game and play to the end on the first try. The fun lies in being challenged, falling down, and figuring out how to work through the obstacles that jump in your way. You try something, you fail, you reboot, and you try again. And you remember exactly what went wrong and build off what you learned. Life is no different.

One of the things I've learned as a professional speaker is this: Trying to be perfect will take you out of the performance.

When it comes to performance, the value that the audience members receive from the substance you share with them is paramount. Now in the past, I would expect perfection. And before every talk, I practice perfecting the pregnant pauses, the power statements, and the narrative from stories that are designed to adhere the audience to me. But I've learned that no matter how well the presentation is received, there's still a flaw somewhere in its composition or delivery. Those who have experience on the stage will relate to this: Whether it's the acoustics, the camerawork, or the seating arrangement, something unexpected will go wrong. As soon as it does, you're going to be stuck in that irritated, frustrated, and emotional state.

When I strive for perfection, the audience might not see it, but I feel it; I know it. I start looking inward and judging my speech. I learned the hard way that trying to be perfect was killing my "good." As humans, we can never be perfect, but in time, we darn sure can be good if we're willing to engage in deliberate practice, welcome constructive critique, and do the work it takes to be better.

There is an *expected range of failure* that is the price of "good." Learn to be okay with it. It will calm your anxiety and turn down the voice of internal doubt. Give that voice even a bit of attention, and it will cue up the song of failure for you. No need to push play on that one!

I have learned through time that we are often our own harshest critics. When that negative voice of doom and gloom starts to whisper and then scream, "You are not good enough! You are not ready! What happens if you screw it up?" you can take your power back. Start to push back and say, "Bull! You're good enough. You're ready. This is what you were born to do; go do it!" This breaks the pattern, and I start to think about what I *will* do, instead of stewing in the adrenaline release of what I *can't* do.

There is an *expected range of failure* if you want to learn a new skill, acquire a new language, prepare for a marathon, start a new job, learn a new dance, create, innovate, or speak in public. Your tolerance range is going to be determined by the value you assign to the endeavor. How bad do you want or need it? Your answer to that question will be the impetus for the next push forward.

Everything is about "next." As you make progress, your disappointment will fade, and what was once anger and frustration will now be channeled into focused and active participation in the quest for improvement. Your expected range of failure will shrink until, and here's the caveat, you push it to the next level. Try something new again, or try to master one of those things that you're already doing.

Don't let your emotions override your expectations. Accept the fact that failure will accompany the next level of achievement. At some point, you'll come to a crossroads of decision. This will be an important choice. You've had some success, and you know that the next level is going to provide an even bigger challenge. This is where most people stop. They compromise their success by labeling it "good enough." How bad do you want success? How bad do you need it? When you raise the stakes to the next level, you'll have answered these questions. The "next level" means a new expected range of failure. You're ready for it; you've been through it before, same steps.

Only the naïve believe they can master something without putting in the work and enduring the sacrifice that mastery demands. You're not naïve. Expect failure, accept it, and then embrace its teachings on the road toward mastery. The only valueless failure is one you refuse to learn from. Be okay with experimentation, and remember that to experiment is to try new things. Some will work; some won't. By trying something that failed, you now know that it doesn't work. You aren't going to waste your time chasing after it again. You are now better able to invest your resources into something else. And if that doesn't work either, you will be that much the wiser. Failure to learn from your mistakes is truly failure. Put in the work, learn from your past, and craft your future.

You can't know or predict all the things that will happen in every situation. You may not be able to see or may be unwilling to acknowledge events that could derail your progress. These events fall into the category of unexpected failures. There will be things that happen outside your span of control, and no matter how perfect your approach, you are destined to fail. Politics get in the way; people change their minds. People want to stay with the mediocrity of the same in a relationship, and no matter how good you look, how well you dress, or how great your program or product is, you'll fail. You don't expect to fail because you've got all the measurables. You never saw it coming, but those things do appear.

Either you didn't want to see it, or you couldn't see it. If you didn't want to see it, that's on you. If you couldn't see it, that might've been something that no one could foresee. But there will be many people with the 20/20 accuracy of hindsight who say, "I told you so." Unexpected failure provides awareness and offers a learning experience.

You will learn from unexpected failure if:

- You leave your ego at the door; get other people involved, and ask them to check out your blind spots.
- You control all the variables you can possibly control. You can only know what you endeavor to find out, and even then, you could be misled, or things can change that you're not aware of.
- You forgive yourself. Don't beat yourself up for things you missed that you couldn't see or know. Statements like "I should've known," "I could've known," or "I should've done this" are revisionist history when it comes to unexpected failure. It's a waste of time and emotion—you need both for your next success.

Creating Value: The Building Blocks of Success

In this book, I have detailed the philosophies, strategies, and tactics that you can apply to learn from failure. You can begin today to use these tools to face, overcome, and rationally create the means and methods to learn from failure as a part of the bargain that success demands.

I will teach you how to turn down the emotional noise that prevents you from logically understanding, strategizing, and approaching your goal from a different angle. You'll be able to spot a mistake you've already made before you repeat the same maneuver and end up with the same result.

No matter how resilient and resourceful you may be, your ability to contain the emotional distress, anxiety, anger, or fear of failure will be directly proportional to the worth you assign to the outcome. Emotion doesn't turn off like a light switch. The residue of regret, rejection, and self-flagellation often accompanies failure.

Failing 1,575 Times per Week

My first job after college was with Liberty Mutual, the insurance company. I was hired for sales.

When I started, the expectation was to get enough leads that would provide enough information to secure appointments in two ways. The first was the tried, true, tested, and often detested cold call. The second was a combination of cold calls with door-to-door selling that included having face-to-face conversations, dropping off a business card, shaking a hand, and dropping off a brochure. Cold calls sting at first, especially if you're not used to rejection.

Cold calls expose your psyche and soul to rejection. I was in the infant stages of constructing a positive, successful orientation. Graduating from college was one small step toward my future success; getting the job with Liberty was the second. Success in this particular job in this industry meant that I had to get used to rejection. Rejection was at the very top of my cycle of avoidance. I would go to great lengths to escape its deflating feeling. But I had to pay the emotional cost, face my fear of rejection, pick up the phone, and attempt to generate interest from a faceless concept of a person.

My first day on the job at Liberty, I was directed to the sales section of the office. There was a ruler in my bullpen desk with the inscription, "Activity Rules Success." I made a commitment to myself to make more cold calls than anyone else in the office. Not just by one or two, but by hundreds. I knew I didn't have the skill set yet to talk about the nuances of the corporate insurance industry, so I had to lean on sheer volume of calls and learn along the way. I would make 350 to 400 calls a day for five days a week. The weekends were spent researching for the calls I would make the next week. On a good week, I would have about a 10 percent success rate of around 35 to 40 people who would have a brief conversation with me. From this brief conversation, 10 percent of these conversations would lead to a meeting.

I was failing upward of 315 times a day, or a whopping 1,575 times per workweek. Ouch! Some of that hurt . . . but only for a while. Because the more I did it, the more my ears were swollen from the pressure of that earpiece, the closer I was getting to a yes. After a while, I learned what worked for me and what didn't. If one approach had a 0 percent success rate, I stopped using it. I started to move off the script the company gave me for those calls, and I began to tweak it with my own style using empathy and humor.

I developed a system to make the calls warmer. I would ask for one thing on each call: permission to send some information for the buyer's review with the promise that if there was no value in the data or verbiage, I would never contact the person again. My success rate in gaining appointments doubled. I was learning from failure. From cold calls, I applied the same techniques and strategies to appointments, closes, and bigger, more sophisticated accounts. I learned early in my career that while product knowledge is essential, self-belief and conviction are vital to your success because they bring vibrancy to the product and form to the process.

I was after success. I had made a commitment to myself, and I was going to do everything in my power to make it happen. For once in my life, success was a nonnegotiable for me.

Rejection is painful. The only way to move through the pain is to partner with it. You partner with pain when you expose yourself to it on a regular basis, using habit and discipline to force yourself through it. You have to expose yourself to your fear. Most of us have a fear of rejection, of showing up "less than" in the eyes of another, a fear of failure. Failure uses rejection as its calling card.

I had to habituate myself to rejection and failure if I was ever going to improve. Habituation is developed through exposure. Habituation is "the diminishing of a physiological or emotional response to a frequently repeated stimulus." You'll assign a value to what you really want, and a corresponding value to what you really fear. You'll find they exist together. Whichever emotion has the stronger pull will determine your course of action. What did I have to lose? I really wanted my success. The more I dialed, the more my confidence grew and the more I began to understand that the nature of interaction on the phone is impersonal. People aren't rejecting me; they're rejecting the concept of me. They were rejecting the approach I was using. I kept on dialing.

The Million-Dollar Call

One of my companies, The Wooditch Group, is an insurance brokerage firm specializing in corporate insurance, worker's compensation, general liability, auto, and coverages germane to a business. Our ascent to success in the industry was rapid. We opened in 1993, and by 1997, we were killing it! But with only a handful of top-gun producers and support from an administrative staff, we needed more service help. We recruited and hired for the position. One of our hires, John B., was finishing college and was looking for a summer job. His attention to detail and his ability to communicate got the attention of his manager, who came to me one day and said, "Do you know how well this person can write? Have you experienced his ability to solve mathematical problems?" I started to pay attention.

John stuck around for about a year before he asked to move into that rarefied air, the money spot: sales. I didn't see how he could make it. I was projecting his ability based on my own bias, my personality, and the personalities of the other producers who were banking the big dollars. He was sophisticated, educated, and analytical, but I couldn't imagine him in sales.

This guy was relentless though. He approached me four times; I finally relented and said, "Okay, write a business plan and bring it to me." What he delivered was, by far, the most comprehensive, well-thought-out business plan I had ever read in my life. I invited him to lunch and laid down the rules of engagement. I said, "I'm going to pay you for one quarter—that's three months—and you're going to have to justify that compensation, or I'm turning off the flow of money, putting you back on the desk, and you will recapture what I paid you."

Later John would tell me this scared the heck out of him. He was like the movie character Zack Mayo in *An Officer and a Gentleman*, doing push-ups in the rain as his drill instructor tried to make him quit. The instructor yelled to him, "Why don't you quit?!" He looked up, almost broken, and said, "I've got nowhere else to go!" And there it is. Deep need, deep desire. No retreat, no surrender.

Let's fast-forward a year later. He justified that salary I paid him in the first couple of months. He did the work. His activity and refined, always-under-construction approach to meeting and securing clients worked. One particular day, he talked with a person that let him know, "There is only a small part of our coverage that is available for you to quote." He found a way to pool his resources and obtain that small portion of the program. Five years later, he wrote the entire account and earned seven figures from that one opportunity that he turned into a cashed result.

Let's dissect what happened in this scenario: He embraced the new; he didn't resist change. He realized that the way forward was to position himself to create his own opportunities. He mastered the nuances of insurance coverage and exhibited the skill set necessary to communicate effectively with people.

At this stage of his career, John could've sought comfort and, in all likelihood, performed at his current level while moving from annual review to annual review all the way up to the top of the chain in our service department. He didn't choose comfort though. He chose risk.

Sales was new to him, so he had to learn by making mistakes. He used our resources and his ability to learn from failure to make fewer and fewer mistakes every day. Agility and adaptability will be two of your keys in learning from failure. When you're not agile, you're stuck in the same mindset, unwilling to adapt. Survival favors those most able to adapt.

So in the midst of failure, ask yourself the following:

- Am I one prospect closer to really making it big? Does failure really hurt that much?
- Am I learning from each failure? Do I have the mindset to follow through on my personal commitment?
- Am I learning how my industry works, and at least the basics to maneuver through and around it?
- And am I in the right place at the right time, a place that supports my attitude and aptitude?

For this book to be of benefit to you, you have to *need* your success. You will have to be emotionally resilient. You will have to be resourceful as you learn to manage the emotional pain of rejection and loss, setback, and failure. It will also be incumbent upon you to define success in your own way, not a cut-and-paste from the thoughts of others. When you learn what it is you truly must have, it will be crucial for you to learn what it is you're willing to give up to obtain it.

Against Average

The ancient Greeks, from the tablets of Aristotle, would tell us that the goal of human thought and action is to flourish, to move beyond happiness. Flourishing demands activity, and if we have the right type of activity, one that is adjusted from missteps, mistakes, and failure, we can pursue a life of flourishing. Think about the term "flourish." Now think about the term "stagnate." People set up camp somewhere between these two extremes.

This book will show you the way to flourish. It will give you the tools to diagnose and approach failure from a rational standpoint. You'll learn the origin of fear, how to work with it and move in spite of it. Once you learn of fear's origins, this book will reveal the way to break the chains of irrational fear and transition to the productivity of rational thought. I'm not going to trick you—it's not easy. It takes work; it's a process.

Our brains are lazy. They prefer to be on autopilot rather than to think critically. The brain also seeks answers to every question. You may know that the answer to your question is illogical, you may not even believe it to your very core, but you put it out there because it makes you feel more certain, safer. Certainty is confinement. You're subjected to what you think you know, and you're not willing to open your mind to something different. It's the same thought process every day, with the expectations of a different result. If you are ready to truly look at your failures, to honestly assess what went wrong and what part you played, and to apply those lessons the next time around, your results will start changing.

Framing Failure

1. **What's the worst that can happen? Identify the worst possible scenario.**
   The first thing you need to do is start thinking about the worst possible thing that can happen. Write it down and make an assessment. Is failure something I will survive? Meaning, "Will it kill me?" If not, what could I lose? Self-esteem, money, time? Could I recover if I lost money? Write down what would happen if everything crashed and burned.

   Give it color—exaggerate the scenarios. You'll start to see a pattern that alleviates your anxiety. Exaggerated scenarios will be so far out (almost like a science fiction movie) that you'll gain perspective.
2. **Expand your choices.**
   Before you dive or step into anything, develop options that address that worst-case scenario. You won't feel

25

trapped with options. One choice is no choice. Stay away from forced choices and develop more options. Ask, "What happens if?" Bullet-point your responses to the question, study them, and then develop options from your responses. Options, options, options. The more, the better!

3. **Labels limit. Don't be so quick to label something as a "failure."**

Success takes time. You're investing in yourself, and often investments take time to yield significant payoffs. Follow your process. If you need to amend your process, then, by all means, make it flexible. But stay engaged with a process. Every action generates a consequence. You have to be able to make an honest assessment. Ask yourself, "Are my actions moving me closer to what I want?" "Closer" is a process that may take weeks, months, or years to develop into success. Be patient, but get moving!

CHAPTER 2

The Greats Have Learned the Art of *Failing More*

Failure is a wonderful teacher. I have failed more times than [every] single person in this room. I promise you, I have failed at more things than any of you. I've written more bad jokes. I flunked out of college. I've been homeless. I lived in a car for three years. Lost everything I have ever owned. Twice. Lost it again in 2005.

I have had a life filled with major league setbacks, but I've learned through all of those setbacks. So, when I make a mistake, I get up and keep going. All of those mistakes are actually valuable experience. Don't let your mistakes define you as a person. You're going to mess up because you need your mess-ups to learn the lesson.

—STEVE HARVEY

Success books are filled with aspirational anecdotes and facts detailing failure-to-success stories from the heroes of history to the provocateurs of the present—from

Lincoln, Churchill, and Edison to Gates, Branson, and Cuban.

If you are determined to share a strand of connective tissue with these greats, then know this: They didn't let failure stop them. They welcomed it; they learned from it; they profited from it. They learned to deal with their fears, and they discovered that the secret to success was in their unwillingness to define failure as fatal, as they clung to their dreams, goals, and aspirations with tenacious resolve.

Failure is a word that lacks power unless you give it meaning and assign an emotional value to it. Failing isn't permanent unless you let it keep you down. When you assign power to the word "failure," you relinquish an equal amount of your power. The emotional weight you assign to failure keeps you down. It drains your energy and depletes the emotional and physical power base you need to succeed.

Just Start!

When Mark Cuban speaks with graduates today, one of the most common questions they ask is what type of work they should engage in. Cuban's universal response is, "You don't need the perfect job. You just need a job—one to learn from." He lets them know that if one job doesn't work out, find another job and then another job until they find something that suits them. This mindset is adaptable; it doesn't strive for perfection. Instead, it encourages the process of learning to find what you are best suited to do at a particular time. Cuban goes on to say, "When you are 22, 23,

24, there is no such thing as failure, really; the point is to get started and learn as much as you can. After all, you're getting paid to learn."

Cuban lives his own advice. After graduating from Indiana University in 1981, he and failure walked hand in hand into corporate America. He started failing from day one. He was fired from his first three jobs, but he was able to pull something from each failure.

According to Cuban, he wasn't into technology in college. He took one computer class and used a method of cheating to get by. But going from classroom theory to real-world application made a difference; one of Cuban's first jobs included technology, and he embraced it. He was in flow, concentrating so hard that he didn't see time flashing by. That's when he realized that he had more than a passing interest. He was emotionally invested, and he thought he could excel with technology. Failure didn't deter him. He looked at it as a bargain that success demands—including an education from its lessons. If he hadn't had those jobs, he never would have experienced what technology could do for him and what he could accomplish once he embraced it. He never would have had the opportunity to find something he loved. He didn't get fired once and then give up on his entire life. He absorbed the lesson and moved to the next job.

Today, Mark Cuban is one of the most recognizable businesspeople in the world. In addition to owning the Dallas Mavericks, a National Basketball Association franchise, he is a star on the ABC reality television show *Shark Tank*.

All You Need Is One Yes

Success is always under construction. It doesn't lend itself to pause, only to action. Fear will hold you back because your brain seeks the comfort of safety.

I like to do the things I'm good at, and when I expand beyond my competency level, my confidence sags a bit. I also don't like the feeling of being uncomfortable. I've learned a lot of lessons about comfort and what you must do to grow beyond the "feel-good" state. The lessons I'll share will take you from the distractions of what you must do to a direction you must take to do it.

Sara Blakely is the founder of Spanx, an apparel company headquartered in Atlanta. Her ascent to prominence includes being recognized by *Time* magazine as one of the 100 most influential people in the world in 2012. In 2014, she was cited by *Forbes* as the ninety-third most powerful woman in the world.

Her father was a trial attorney, and upon graduation from Florida State, she had designs to follow in his footsteps. One of the criteria for admission to law school is the LSAT (Law School Admission Test). After receiving low scores, she made a radical career pivot to a job at Walt Disney World in Orlando. Humor is an important part of life if you're going to maintain a semblance of sanity. Facing one the greatest fears we have as humans, public speaking, she auditioned for the job of stand-up comedian and performed at Disney World for the next three months.

After her stint with Disney, she moved on to selling fax machines. She took the people and customer service skills she learned at Disney and applied them to her sales pitch. Sara's sales results earned her a promotion to a national sales trainer at the age of 25.

But Florida's heat and humidity was not conducive to wearing pantyhose all day. Plus, Sara disliked the look of the pantyhose she was forced to wear. But she did appreciate that the control-top model eliminated panty lines and made her body appear to be firmer. So she experimented and cut off the feet of the pantyhose and found that even with the hose rolling up her legs, she created the look she wanted. (You can find those original pants at the Spanx headquarters.)

By age 27, she was still working in sales, but she had relocated to Atlanta. By this time, she had also dumped some of her savings into the development of her hosiery idea. One day, Sara made the six-hour drive to North Carolina, the capital of America's hosiery mills, primed with enthusiasm to sell her idea. She was turned down by everyone she met. Established companies often default to "safe" when selecting their partners or vendors. Making a maverick selection doesn't get anyone fired, but then there is limited or no progress. The people she met with were unable or unwilling to see the value in her concept.

But all you need to begin your climb to success is one yes, and it all begins with the first step. Roughly two weeks after returning to Atlanta, she received a call from a mill operator in Asheboro, North Carolina. He expressed support for her idea because his three daughters loved the concept.

And from the flames of failure, Spanx was created. The company grossed $4 million in sales in its first year in business and $10 million in its second. Today, Sara Blakely has a net worth of $1.14 billion. She believed in her product, she found the need, and she pursued her dream. And she didn't let her past failures get in her way. She didn't stop adapting after law school didn't pan out. Low LSAT scores, her short time as a comedienne, the customer service lessons she took away from Disney, and the money she earned in sales worked together to make this happen. The rest is, as they say, an American success story.

The G.O.A.T.

"Activity rules success" is an axiom that extends to all parts of life, and especially that microcosm of life that is sport. Sports are a window that reflects our struggles, triumphs, pains, gains, wins, and losses. Some of us choose to stay on the sidelines, as spectators, while others engage as active participants.

Embracing rejection and failure as a way to success is perhaps best illustrated by the exemplar of greatness in sport, Michael Jordan (the G.O.A.T., or Greatest of All Time).

His object lesson about the symbiosis between failure and success can be found in countless corporate and locker-room settings. "I've missed more than 9,000 shots in my career. I've lost almost 300 games. 26 times, I've been trusted to take the game-winning shot, and missed. I've failed over and over and over again in my life. And that is why I succeed."

How would you like your failures to be under the glare of a national spotlight? Imagine the entire nation tuning in to watch your sales pitch fall flat, and the cameras follow you out of the office, while expletives fill the air, and tears of rejection fill your eyes.

The pain of failure can be used for the fuel of forward progress if you find a way to channel it constructively. Jordan took that pain, and he used it to improve his game.

Imagine his disappointment, the abject feeling of failure, when in 1978, as a sophomore in high school, he tried out for his varsity basketball team and didn't make it. It wasn't talent; it was politics, size, and strategy.

When politics intervene, you're subject to forces beyond your control. This is one of those harsh yet constant realities of life. Politics often lurk in the shadows in business and sport. There will also be times when you won't be able to win because your strategy is ineffective. Once you remove yourself from the emotional sting of disappointment, you can adjust, adapt, and win the next day. As we learned in Chapter 1, you can only control so many variables. Some are outside your span of influence.

When Jordan found out that the one open roster spot on the varsity team went to his friend, he was emotionally devastated. He locked himself in his room and began to cry uncontrollably. He was so heartbroken that he wanted to give up the sport. Now, his friend didn't have Jordan's talent, but what he did have was size. In his socks, Jordan was a mere 5 feet 10 inches at the time, and it seems size mattered to that team. I wonder what the coach would think later when Jordan grew from 5 foot 10 to 6 foot 6 and into the stratosphere of legend!

Support and encouragement are requisite conditions that most of us need to pick ourselves up from failure. Michael's champion was his mother, who would intervene and encourage him to weather the storm and to maintain a steadfast belief in himself while passionately pursuing his dreams. From this experience, a recurring pattern in Jordan's life was indelibly etched in his psyche. Failure would result in more effort. It would be his fuel. He would take losses personally and hold on to them. There was a fire in his belly that accompanied the pain of failure. He held the lessons of failure up close and personal and let them simmer inside him until he expelled them in the arena of his profession. His achievement was on the other side of failure—two sides of the same coin.

From the depths of disappointment and that tear-stained pillow, Michael Jordan would matriculate at North Carolina, which had a blue-chip basketball program. In the pressure cooker that was the 1982 NCAA Championship, Jordan drained the winning shot to beat Georgetown. On the court that night, it must have seemed to him as if that high school rejection was worlds away. Later, drafted by the Chicago Bulls, he would lead them to six NBA championships.

The story doesn't end with Jordan hoisting his sixth championship trophy either. There's more failure left in his legacy.

Frustration and loss went hand in hand when Michael Jordan became the owner of the NBA's Charlotte Bobcats.

The Bobcats immediately bled red ink, and Jordan had to put his own money in just to cover operating expenses. Watching the Bobcats go 7 and 59 in his first season (an NBA record for failure) had to feel to Jordan like a knife twisting slowly into his emotional center. The team lacked community support and was a metaphor for dysfunction. Even the glow of Michael Jordan couldn't put a shine on that mess!

The shorter the distance between a thought you know you must act upon and its immediate action, the greater the chance of your success in the endeavor. Jordan immediately jumped into the messy fray and took action. He looked back to move forward. He brought in an LA Lakers assistant coach to replace the previous one, and in probably the most difficult thing he's ever done in his life, he removed himself from the team's operations, taking his ego out of the equation. He knew that being a part of the action was what he wanted, but it wasn't helping his team. As hard as it was, he dissected the season's failures and saw himself as part of the cause. No matter how much that must have hurt, he knew he had to take a back seat. That brutal honesty paid off, and the changes made a big difference.

Often, the difficult pill to swallow is that you are the obstacle on your road to success. I can't tell you how many times I've had to remove myself from the negotiation table or accept the fact that I didn't have what it took to accomplish what needed to be done. The key is, you have to see it first, then accept it, and finally have the courage to exit stage left. Imagine how difficult it must've been for Jordan, Mr. Basketball, who probably just wanted to pick up the ball and do it himself.

As an owner, when the collective success of your enterprise exceeds your personal attachment to the achievement, you foster esprit de corps and build the foundation for sustainable advancement. The next year, the Bobcats finished 43 and 49 and made the playoffs. Public interest increased, and so did ticket sales. The team became profitable. Into the black, out of the red! If Jordan had been reluctant to examine what was causing his team to fail, if he had walked away from that first season having learned nothing, he would have been doomed to repeat that season in perpetuity. But he had the strength to take himself out of the equation, and it worked.

Find Your Center

Elizabeth Gilbert wrote the world-famous book *Eat, Pray, Love*. It was a huge literary success that attracted ardent fans of both her writing and the story. As she began to write her second book, she felt trepidation and uncertainty. The book would be a departure from *Eat, Pray, Love*, and she feared that her fans would be disappointed with the product.

Gilbert thought she had to find a way to her center. As much as she feared alienation from her fans and a lack of acceptance by the general public for her next book, she feared to limit her expression more. It was her expression that made her unique and gave her an endearing voice, while being a powerful beacon of possibility. She looked back at the past few years of her life and thought about what "being successful" really meant to her. She realized that success wasn't writing a bestseller that became a blockbuster movie. Success was being true to herself and expressing herself on her terms. At her core, she found something that she loved more than herself or her ego— her writing. That was her center, and that brought her back to what she called her "home."

Her advice: Go home to your center. Your center is that "thing" that takes your ego out of the equation. It shouldn't be for money, love, or fame. It can't be because you fear what others will say. Instead, you do it because it is the truest expression of you.

To paraphrase Gilbert when she speaks about success and failure during her 2014 Ted Talk titled "Your Elusive Creative Genius":

> Think of it like this: For most of your life, you live out your existence here in the middle of the chain of human experience, where everything is normal and reassuring and regular, but failure catapults you abruptly way out over here into the blinding darkness of disappointment. Success catapults you just as abruptly but just as far way out over here into the equally blinding glare of fame and recognition and praise. And one of these fates is objectively seen by the world as bad, and the other one is objectively seen by the world as good, but your subconscious is completely incapable of discerning the difference between bad and good.

Past successes don't ensure future ones, and the pressure to re-create results can easily stop you from moving forward. Remember, you don't just learn from your failures; you learn from your successes as well. For Gilbert, looking back and redefining what it meant to be successful allowed her to move forward with the next project without worrying what would happen when it was published. Fear of failure doesn't just lead to failure; it leads to stagnation. Don't allow your past—be it good or bad—to dictate your future.

Framing Failure

1. **You don't need a perfect job; you just need a job to learn from.**
   When you learn, you'll become of value. When you become of value, you'll be recruited for your ideal job.
2. **You'll miss 100 percent of the shots you don't take.**
   When you miss, shoot. If you miss again, shoot again until you make it! This is a metaphor for the attempts it takes at times to make it in life.
3. **Find your center.**
   Failure and success can pull you into the vast wilderness where you think that one is fatal and the other final. Find what you love, work from your center, and you will maintain your balance without regard to the critics or the applause.

CHAPTER 3

Recognize Fear

Nothing in life is to be feared.
It is only to be understood.
Now is the time to understand
more, so that we may fear less.

—MARIE CURIE

E xamining our failures rationally is not an easy thing to do. Accepting reality means taking a hard look at your mistakes, owning them, and creating a new plan of attack to make your next approach more effective. Look at it this way: You're still standing, which means you have the opportunity to analyze, make corrections, and then move forward from the direction of failure's teaching. The fact that you are still here also means that you have one less reason to fear failure. It didn't kill you. Now you can use it to make you stronger.

The first demand of success is for you to recognize that fear is holding you back from its promise. You can't achieve and sustain success until you learn to overcome fear's attempts to stop you in your tracks. In this chapter, I'm going to help you shine the light of awareness on fear. You'll find out where it comes from and what it's designed to do. You'll also learn how to recognize the difference between rational and imagined fears.

In addition, you'll be given the tools you need to recognize the type of fear that's holding you back. You will learn that procrastination, lack of prioritization, and the absence of goals all have their origins in fear. Unless you understand the origin of your fears and summon the courage to face them, they will become a wildfire that engulfs your life and leaves your dreams in ashes.

Anything in life of merit or value comes at a cost, with a sacrifice, and often with the clear and present possibility of failure. Refusal to acknowledge or engage in those activities that include the potential of failure means you're playing it safe. You play it safe because you fear. Fear can sabotage your career and marginalize your life. Your dreams and aspirations for a better life can only become your lived reality when you recognize that fear is the ultimate dream killer.

You're Not Alone

Everyone feels fear. Fear makes us feel uncomfortable. And who doesn't crave comfort? Who doesn't seek a sanctuary of safety in a world fraught with uncertainty? We need fear, but we need to learn how to use it to our advantage. Because, after all, fear can be a protective ally or a forbidding adversary. In both cases, it is the first and most formidable obstacle to success.

You tell yourself you're committed. You tell yourself you're "ready to go." You tell yourself you're going to do what it takes to make it. But are you making a wish or a commitment? If you're ready to make a commitment, is it nonnegotiable? Nonnegotiable means there is no settling, no rationalized compromise, or anything less than making your intended result a reality. To earn the result, there's a pain threshold that you're going to have to cross to do what you must to achieve your goal. Pain is relative. It regulates on an individual sliding scale between how much you need to have success and how much you are willing to personally invest in the outcome.

Maybe you're qualified for the promotion you want to ask for, or maybe you want to submit your résumé for a new job, but something makes you stall. That "something" is fear—you don't feel you're good enough or are worried that you'll be rejected. You don't even try for the position, and you end up losing by default. You're capable of going after that bigger, more lucrative business deal, but you don't think you have the right stuff to play at that higher level of competition. You assume those people who compete at the higher echelon are more deserving of the opportunity—smarter, faster, bigger, and better. So you play small and stay safe. Your fixed mindset will yield a scarcity of opportunity and a reward commensurate with the limits of your thinking.

Or maybe you've achieved some success, but your ego is now wrapped around your accomplishments. You opt for the comfort of a maintenance phase, unaware that trying to maintain stasis will foster the conditions for regression.

Either you're moving forward, or you're regressing. That's physics. You can't stay in the same place, thinking you are hermetically sealed in a vacuum of time and space. In every case, it's fear that's holding you back.

Fear prevents you from making the attempts that continual improvement mandates. It is the obstacle that prevents your success. Fear isn't a zero-sum game. Each of us feels it; it just varies by degree and nature. At stake is the difference between a life you earn by acknowledging, accepting, and moving through your fear and a life where you settle for mere existence. Failure to recognize and move through fear rationalizes the excuses that will marginalize your life. Achievement is "next-level" stuff. You conquer the molehill; then you learn what it takes to scale the mountain.

Where Fear Originates

When imagined fear overwhelms you, it is important to recognize that fear originates from two sources: an avoidance of loss or an aversion to change. Once you understand where your fears originate, you can then weigh the course of action necessary to achieve your goals. Be forewarned though, if you're going to achieve your goals, you will have to act in ways that are contrary to your brain's preference for safety. And the more audacious the goal, the more likely the chance of failure. Get used to it—nothing worthy or of value was ever created without dissecting failure's lessons.

As a teenager, I would walk three miles down alleyways and through what my family and friends labeled a "bad neighborhood" to get to school. As I entered an alley or walked through that bad neighborhood, the hairs on my neck and arms would stand up. My amygdala was on alert for danger. Sometimes it came in the form of bullies who would trap me in an alley or stray dogs that would chase me down the street.

One day, the bullies found me. I was nine at the time.

The image from that day is still etched vividly in my mind. It changed the rest of my life. I was wearing my prized birthday possession, my brand-new baseball hat with a small plastic baseball sewn on the front.

I can still remember those ornate, beveled stones that decorated the exterior of the church I was passing when the incident happened. The bullies pounced from the shadows, the sounds of half-empty beer cans hitting the pavement. The chase began. My legs were churning as I was running as fast as I could. There was a small enclave carved out of the church's facade. I ran into that enclave and was trapped. I remember the hat being torn off my head. Time was suspended as I watched the miniature baseball bounce around between the stones on the ground.

There were laughs, taunts, threats, and anger in the faces and words of my tormentors. I ran home with the little baseball in my hand. My shirt was torn, my hat was crumpled, and my heart was racing.

My 6-foot, 3-inch authoritarian Pennsylvania State Police trooper father was in the garage when I arrived. As usual, he was covered in sawdust, as woodworking was his passion and pastime. He looked up and surveyed my torn and frayed clothing.

"Dad, Dad, they beat me up!" My father leveled a serious look at me, then offered a lecture and lesson: "Son, you can keep running from the bully, but one day you will run out of room. When you run out of room, you will have to make a choice. You can cower in the corner from fear, or you can stand, plant your feet, and face it."

Head down, heaving and sobbing, I walked out of the garage and sat down under the massive weeping willow in the backyard. (In hindsight, what an appropriately named tree!) The tears flowed freely as I imagined the future pain of getting beat up. I imagined my knees shaking as I stood my ground. I realized I was alone. There would be no one to "fight my fights" anymore. I had to face the bullies in my life head-on. No retreat, no surrender.

As my emotions subsided, I started to think. I didn't recognize it at the time, but my father was shifting my attention from fear to rational thought. Those tears dried up as I looked inside myself to find the true nature of my character. As a child, your character is malleable. It's formed and tested by those bullies, physical or imagined, that chase you, shame you, and sometimes beat you up.

I wish I knew then what I know now. Under the branches of that tree, I was forming the basis of a survival mindset that would require both the physical and the mental to implement. I would look back years later and think of my father in his garage. The lesson I learned that day in between the tears and the sawdust would become an enduring, valuable companion on my way forward.

Fear as Procrastination

Without goals, you have no direction or destination. When you put pen to paper and inscribe those goals in your journal, realize that an unwritten challenge will accompany each goal. Put your pen down; heed your call to action. Get ready—action engenders those twin echoes of fear: emotional uncertainty and the feeling of loss.

Once you recognize that it's fear that is stopping you, you have an obligation to locate the source of your fear and find a way to move forward in spite of it. You don't negotiate with it; you find a way to accept the uncertainty that accompanies the feeling of failure instead. Fear disguises itself as procrastination or distraction. You think to yourself, "I'm not ready. It's not the perfect time. I'm not good enough. I'll be better tomorrow."

Every day, you engender or encounter distractions. Distractions derail or defer the direct-line pursuit and obtainment of your goal. It's the salesperson who, instead of making cold calls, creates files, rearranges the office space daily, takes an hour in the break room before, during, and after lunch, and then performs like a dilettante, not a professional. Dilettantes have a passing interest; professionals are invested in the outcome. Hours go by; momentum is lost. And as the hours sweep by, so goes the day, the month, and the year.

Most fail to recognize that it's irrational fear that holds them back in life. We tend to blame external obstacles for our internal unwillingness to put ourselves in play. The things in life that are of value and critical to our success will bring us up close and personal with the very real prospect of failure. But how do you recognize that it's fear that's stopping you? First, let's draw the distinction between fear and danger.

Distinguishing Between Fear and Danger

Fear is a primal emotion. Your survival instincts are hardwired into your nervous system. Your ability to distinguish between rational and irrational fear will provide a guide to understanding what can cause physical harm and what is a product of your overactive imagination.

Rational fear is the early warning system that alerts you to danger. Danger presents itself from people, reptiles, and insects—real and often immediate threats to our survival. It warned early humans of imminent danger from animals, other humans, or insects. Today, there is no sabertooth tiger in our conference or living room.

Conversely, irrational fear is a product of your imagination. When you perceive a "threat" and project future harm, your body reacts in the same way as it does to real danger. This fight, flight, or freeze response is a product of your genetic imprint. Today's sabertooth tiger of your imagination can be an angry client or spouse, or it might be a deadline you're running up against. All are socially learned fears. We live in an evolved world of rockets, electric cars, and all the comforts that Amazon can provide with a click, but our survival mechanism is still back in the caves and on the plains.

Today, we're still hardwired to survive the predators our ancestors fought off enabling our survival. Our minds and bodies are often at odds. Our natural instinct informs us to run or fight, but our subconscious can't distinguish between the various types of confrontational experiences we face today. Instinct drives us down and back into the reptile brain.

Fear holds us hostage in a cycle of adrenaline release. The more dangerous the perceived situation, the bigger the buildup and release of adrenaline. Unutilized, adrenaline demands an outlet, and that unspent surge often results in anxiety and, left unchecked, the "black dog" of depression. When we begin to fear fear itself, the trickle of adrenaline is released from the imagined consequences of confrontation. We feel out of control and helpless and caught up in a web of fear and adrenaline.

What Keeps You Up at Night?

Hypothetical scenarios create panic, and panic perpetuates feelings of fear and the release of adrenaline. This cycle of adrenaline release resulting in fear is physically and mentally debilitating. There is a way to stop the cycle. To do this, we need to understand the difference between being aware of fear and accepting it. Let's look at each:

- BE AWARE. Become acquainted with the feeling. Fear is a feeling. It holds as much power over you as you permit. Be aware that what you're feeling is human.
- ACCEPT IT. By accepting fear, you lessen its power. Expect it because it's never going away; then embrace and welcome the feelings that accompany it. I know this sounds crazy, but when you welcome the inevitable, you steal its power. When you expect it, you're prepared for it. Make a pact with yourself: "I can live with this." By making this statement, you take back your power—and you need this power to perform at your best.

To sum it up, start becoming more aware and accept fear, and you will break the cycle of fear, adrenaline, fear, adrenaline.

Irrational fears lack the foundation of reality. Learning to control and minimize these fears is a part of the nonnegotiable requirement that living a successful life demands. It's critical to recognize the type of fear that is holding you back. Is it a physical threat to your body? Or is it a blow to your self-esteem, confidence, and ego? Learning the difference will determine the direction in which you need to dispatch or limit the fear that is preventing you from moving forward.

Craving Certainty

Certainty is brain candy—your brain craves it. But I have found that certainty often comes at the cost of a biased perspective. Generating assumptions that form entrenched conclusions, it hardens your mind to anything that runs counter to your confirmation bias. Confirmation bias rules the brain's need for certainty—and you tend to interpret new information as a confirmation of your existing belief.

Most of the time, I work with my nature, but there are times when I need to work against my brain's craving for certainty. Of course, I have the same need to ask why. But with the tools of awareness and discipline, the question is much quieter. I no longer ask why. I've avoided the slippery slope of supposition by training my brain to not seek certainty in "certain" things.

The first part of training is to be aware of what it is you're training. In this case, I'm training my brain to stop doing what it's genetically programmed to do. The brain's primary function is to preserve itself, and it seeks protection through answers. Answers provide certainty, even if—and this is crucial—we know we're feeding ourselves far-fetched ideas or concepts.

- MINDSET—be aware that you're working against your natural inclination to find certainty in everything. You know you're succumbing to your nature when you start making up scenarios or drawing conclusions about those issues for which you have no concrete facts. You're making suppositions that could lead to failure

49

because you have no factual direction, only the ambiguous route of "guesswork."

- MANAGEMENT—monitor your self-talk. Catch yourself trying to make up an answer instead of endeavoring to know the facts. Check your facts and go forward on the basis of your findings.

The Roads of Fear

Let's take a walk down the high and low roads of the fear response.

Let's start with the *low road*, which is the direct route to our brain stem, or our instincts. If you're walking down the street and you see someone brandishing a weapon, your senses direct you down the low road of survival mode, because this is a life-threatening situation. The thalamus, which receives signals from your senses, sends a signal to the amygdala. From there, the amygdala sends signals to your hypothalamus, which fires up your adrenal glands and pumps blood to your muscles. The flow of chemicals and blood creates the fight, flight, or freeze response that has enabled our survival as a species.

The *high road* is a non-life-threatening event where the amygdala sends signals to the prefrontal cortex, also referred to as our rational brain. This part of our brain alerts the hippocampus, which is our memory center, and makes an immediate determination about the nature of the threat.

You take the high road when you bring discernment into the fear response by engaging your prefrontal cortex, or rational brain. By doing this, you calm the sympathetic survival instinct. When you calm the sympathetic response, you enter into the parasympathetic rest phase where cortisol subsides, and you can gain the essential homeostasis that is your system's way of providing balance to the unrest and upheaval that can occur from the release of cortisol.

Excessive cortisol levels wreak havoc on your immune system, and sustained high levels kill brain cells and other vital organs. Cortisol overload will decrease your muscle mass and engender premature aging. Some experts have termed cortisol the "death hormone," because it's associated with old age and disease. Remember, you need it for short bursts, but a prolonged release is not good for you.

The 6 Inches Between Your Ears

Perhaps the masters of mindset are those who live or die within the 6 inches between their ears, the Navy SEALs. I was humbled and honored to be exposed to this mindset during my interview with Navy SEAL Andy Stumpf, who offered this pragmatic philosophy on failure: "It's not a matter of if you're going to fail; it's a matter of when it's going to happen, and what you are going to do about it."

Sirius XM Radio is a broadcast company that provides three satellite and online radio services operating in the United States, with an estimated audience of 32 million. When I was presented with the opportunity to host my own show, I jumped at the chance.

The Bill Wooditch Show aired Saturday nights at 6:05 p.m. PST.

My assistant, Kelsey McDaniel, produced the Sirius format. She would connect with our broadcast station and facilitate the inbound calls from listeners. She used a problem-shooting checklist and assumed responsibility for the stewardship of a glitch-free show. But there was never a glitch-free show. We lived Murphy's law every Saturday. Whether it was a guest calling in on a cell phone with a low signal, our producers in Dallas not getting our voice modulation right, or commercial breaks starting without warning, something went wrong every time.

The show was gaining momentum, and the final episode of our Sirius season was with a person I looked forward to not only interviewing but meeting.

We convinced a Navy SEAL to come up from San Diego and do the show live in our studio, which was my home library reconfigured with monitors, speakers, computers, glaring lights, and a whiteboard.

Andy Stumpf knocked on my door 40 minutes before showtime. Some of the conversations that occur before the microphones go on are the best material. I can tell you without compromising his trust—this guy is the real deal.

Kelsey was at my house an hour before the show. On a good day, she needed five minutes to set up. However, today she had a fever and wanted to make darn sure we didn't revisit Murphy's law. We were set up and ready to go 45 minutes before we were due to air. Everything was perfect. Andy and I took our seats in the studio, the production crew in Dallas was ready, and our cue, which was

60 seconds of the song "The Final Countdown" until we went live, began. And then, just as it was going so well, we cut to black. There was a power outage in a 20-mile radius around our home base. This time, no rewiring, pushing, plugging, or restarting was going to save us.

I tried to remain calm. While Kelsey was turning a lighter shade of pale, Sirius started to air an old show of mine as I sat there in embarrassment, frustration, and anger. But Andy was calm and composed. Whether it was divine intervention or nimble hands inserting the proper plug into the right socket, 15 minutes later we had power! Our producer's voice carried a cautiously optimistic tone as he asked, "Bill? Bill, are you there?" I was, and soon enough we were under way.

Throughout the entire interview, Andy was calm, collected, eloquent, and engaging. I segued from some general questions about life into the emotion of combat. We got into real "boots on the ground" stuff—from extended boredom to the horror and extreme terror of firefights.

During the interview, Andy transitioned between the experience he endured as a SEAL trainee and the experience he delivered as an instructor. He found that taking on the role of instructor was a vastly different experience from his harsh indoctrination as a student.

Each day, Andy had the opportunity to either find a way to make it to the next meal or *fail*. He had to break down the day into small chunks to survive. Even though Andy's lifelong goal was to become a Navy SEAL, he couldn't focus on the end; he had to remain centered in the present, breaking down each physically and mentally challenging event into small increments. Conversely, the instructor tries to overwhelm the student with the totality of the negative experience, saying things like, "This is going to be every day for the rest of your training. Every day, you're going to be in this cold water, running in sand, and doing things until you drop."

You may be overwhelmed by the demands of your goal, to the point where the expanse of frustration and energy expenditure just doesn't seem worth the effort. You may reach the point where you just want to ring the bell and give up on *your* lifelong goal. Like the Navy SEALs, you can't get emotional; you have to stay centered in logic and break things down to small wins every day.

This is a mindset that can keep you alive in business and on the battlefield. I asked Andy about the emotional highs and lows of combat. "You can't get emotional in combat," he said, unemotionally. "If you do, you die. You have to stay within that 6 inches between your ears where logic, reason, and critical thinking come into play." It's the small wins that inch you toward the realization of your goals. Remain anchored in logic and stay within the 6 inches between your ears.

Will You Ring the Bell?

Failure is going to happen. The big question is what will you do when it does? Will you ring your own metaphorical bell and quit? Or will you maintain the pursuit of your goal, and stay anchored to a mindset that isn't overwhelmed by inevitable setbacks that are a part of daily life? Unless you're trying to become a Navy SEAL, you'll likely experience fear that comes from not wanting to risk your self-esteem. You care too much about what other people think, and that makes you emotional. Once you start responding to the external, you lose and they win. The game is over.

Your success is up to *you*. Your duty is to get out of that negative field of emotion and start thinking rationally.

Andy's story is a great example of expressed commitment to "make it" and the separation of those who do and those who don't—all due to the 6 inches between your ears.

Social Fears

As babies, we're born with only two fears: the fear of falling and the fear of loud noises. All other fears are socially learned. While you may never completely unlearn your social fears, you can deal with them once you understand their origin. This awareness is the first step in understanding the difference between danger and imagined fear.

The second step is to rationally make a decision to make a change. At this stage, ask yourself this question: If everything goes up in flames, what's the worst that can happen? Know it, protect it, and then develop the means and methods to create your upside.

Own this as your personal nonnegotiable: If you are ever to achieve the success you seek, you must first be able to differentiate between irrational fear and real danger. Once you draw the distinction, you have an obligation to act on that which you have learned.

Framing Failure

1. **Don't let fear prevent your success.**
   Fear prevents you from making those attempts that continual improvement mandates. Recognizing the source of your fear is the first step in facing it. When you face it, you'll be met with a decision. At stake is the difference between life and existence. The former is earned by facing fear and moving through it, and the latter is a surrender to existence through fear avoidance.

2. **Learn which particular fear is causing your inertia.**
   We are the sum of our fears, and some of our fears are greater than the rest. First, you need to identify which fear is causing your delay. Exposure to your fear will lessen its severity. Start with small steps but expose yourself to your fear.

3. **Once you've learned which fear is holding you back, you need to move through it.**
   Fear or need—whichever is the stronger emotion—will compel your direction. Either you'll shrink up, make excuses, and create conditions and obstacles, or you'll look in the mirror, understand the origin of your fear, face it, and make it happen.

4. **Learn the difference between rational and irrational fear.**

   Rational fear is the early warning system that alerts you to danger. Irrational fear is a product of your imagination. You perceive a "threat," you project a future harm, and your body reacts in the same way as it does to real danger.

5. **Learn that procrastination, distraction, and rationalization are conditions you create because you fear failure.**

   It is tempting to tell yourself, "I'm not ready," or "It's not the perfect time," or "I'm not good enough. I'll be better tomorrow." Don't believe these lies. You're ready. There is no perfect time. You are good enough to start, and you'll be better tomorrow for starting today.

6. **Know that there can't be sustainable success in the absence of failure.**

   You meet success on its terms and conditions, and you'll find its demands are nonnegotiable. The first condition of success is failure. No sustainable success can occur before failure. None. No matter how much you "want" it, no matter how much you "need" it, the ultimate measure of want and need is accepting failure as a part of the process that winning demands.

7. **Negative imprints can leave an indelible impression.**

   We tend to carry emotional baggage with us, and some of that weight is the negative experiences of others that we project onto ourselves. We're burdened with our own fear and the fear of following in the footsteps of others who have failed in relationships or business.

Perhaps your fear of divorce is a product of your parents' failed marriage.

Awareness and visualization can help you navigate your past. You lose your power for change when you believe the past will determine your future. The past can be a guide, but it doesn't have to be a dictator driving you from what you want by making you fear those things that have already happened.

CHAPTER 4

Break Through
the Obstacles
That Limit Success

*My upbringing allowed me to be comfortable
with failure. The one trait in a lot of dyslexic
people I know is that by the time we got out
of college, our ability to deal with failure
was very highly developed. And so, we look
at most situations and see much more of the
upside than the downside. Because we're so
accustomed to the downside. It doesn't faze
us. I thought about it many times, I really
have, because it defined who I am. I wouldn't
be where I am today without my dyslexia.
I never would've taken that first chance.*

—GARY COHN

Gary Cohn grew up in Cleveland, Ohio, a product of
the 1960s, with middle-class values and a blue-collar
work ethic. As a child, Cohn was diagnosed with dyslexia.
By forced choice, he attended many schools, most of which
had no clue about how to deal with his condition. "If you're

really fortunate, and work really hard with him," one of his teachers said, "at best, he might grow up to be a truck driver."

As Cohn was spinning his wheels without much result and trying to keep his head above water in school, his brothers became actively involved in his studies. This was hard work, as it took 22 hours for Cohn to read six pages. Persistence, when directed with an adherence to the fundamentals of learning, can create opportunity previously unavailable. After graduating from high school, Cohn earned the opportunity to enroll at American University. Sadly, no employers were lining up to hire Cohn after graduation. But it was okay since Cohn seemed to have his own success niche already picked out—he had a burning interest to become involved in the financial markets. Pipe dreams are fantasies without the possibility of fruition, and the idea that Cohn would actually be involved in a white-collar business seemed to be exactly that—a dream. So, due to an obligation to please his father, he stayed close to home and got a job with United States Steel in Akron, Ohio, where he sold aluminum siding and window frames.

If Cohn would've stayed in Akron and sold aluminum siding, he still would've been a tremendous success, but he wanted more.

There's something in the DNA of high achievers. You see it and you feel it when you're around them. They have a drive, the need for the next thing. They're constantly on the "always-forward" quest for self-improvement. Well, Cohn had the DNA, and one day while visiting the company's office on Long Island right outside New York City, he asked his manager for a day off, and he ventured to Wall Street, walking through the epicenter of the financial district. Spotting a well-dressed man getting into a cab, Cohn asked if he could share it with him. As fortune would have it, this man was a Wall Street executive. His firm had just launched its options business, which he told Cohn, "Frankly, none of us know anything about it." Cohn's response was pure prevarication. He blurted, "I know everything about options!"

By the time Cohn got out of the taxi, he had asked for and received his ridesharing companion's phone number. As Cohn recalls, "He said, 'Call me Monday.'" Cohn made the call, flew back to New York for an interview that week, and started work the Monday after. Now it was time for Cohn to cash that check of promise and actually learn what he claimed to master. Before starting, he read McMillon's *Options as a Strategic Investment*. His first job was as a runner on the trading floor.

Hungry, poor, and determined, Cohn excelled, and in 1990, Goldman Sachs recruited Cohn. This was the beginning of a career that spanned over two decades with the bank. In 1994, his career on the rise, Cohn became a partner in the firm. One of his many defining moments came when he let his boss know that he couldn't quite balance trading and managing. In what was either abdication, frustration, or both, the manager said, "Figure it out," and hung up on him. This became yet another obstacle to be overcome on his march to continued success.

It didn't take Cohn long to swing into action. He called his department into the conference room and made the pronouncement, "I will no longer trade anything." This was the right move.

After a 27-year career, Cohn could look back on what he achieved with deep satisfaction. Besides himself and family, no one believed in him. He was laser-focused on his dream, and he was deaf to the naysayers and doubters who told his parents that, at best, all he would ever be was a truck driver. He was stronger than the obstacle that, to Cohn, was simply a challenge to be overcome on the way to his dream.

Gary didn't fear failure. This was a product of overcoming his learning disability, which gave him the courage he needed to take chances. Some of us are faced with obstacles that may seem daunting. These obstacles can be a forum for excuses or a surrender to conditions if we renounce our personal responsibility to overcome them. We can overcome these obstacles if we don't fear failure and we put in the work it takes to achieve in spite of the size or nature of the impediment.

This chapter will teach you how to live without the fear of failure. Once you understand and rid yourself of the fear of trying something and falling short, you will be able to open doors you never even considered knocking on before.

How Do I Overcome This Obstacle?

Uncertainty and fear are the foremost obstacles to risk taking. Each of us has a specific genetic wiring, a neural circuitry that equips us to deal with uncertainty. Your response to failure is a product of past experiences and the lessons gained from those setbacks. The question is, how do you handle things? Are you more comfortable with the risk? Did you learn from your failure? Have you been able to distance yourself from the emotional pain? Are you now ready to use logic and make a more informed attempt from failure to create a positive outcome?

When you move from emotion (fear) to logic (obstacle management), you can then visualize an outcome by walking through the imaginary steps it takes to achieve it. You have the lessons of failure at your disposal. Now you can rationally use them to avoid the pitfalls that you previously encountered. This is one of the gifts of failure: the ability to anticipate through logic and visualization. Anticipation asks the question, "How do I overcome this obstacle?"

The following quote from Dr. David Baskin, a neuro-surgeon at Houston Methodist Hospital, as relayed to Kayt Sukel for her book *The Art of Risk*, underscores the importance of visualization and success:

I look at the films. I look at MRI scans. I carefully consider the patient's history and physical examination. And then I think about how I'm going to approach the tumor. While doing that, I'll ask myself, "What are the four or five things that could go wrong?" And if those things go wrong, "What am I going to do about it?" This becomes second nature with experience, but I think that, no matter how experienced you are, you need to mentally prepare yourself for those high-risk things, because these are high-risk surgeries. By definition, unexpected and potentially catastrophic events are going to occur. You need to be prepared to deal with them. You need to set your expectations. And you need to visualize a clear path to success.

Low Ceilings

Maybe you've been told since childhood that you weren't good enough. Maybe the ceilings of expectation in your household, school, or town were low. These barriers were constructed for those who wanted to play it safe and simply get through the day. As a boy, if I jumped as high as I could, I could touch the ceilings of my house with my fingertips—and I can't jump, so you get the idea.

Most kids believe their dad is "Superman," and during my childhood, I was no different. Despite my father's fearlessness and strength, I never actually expected him to be Superman. It was *his* expectations for *me*. He expected *me* to be a perfect iteration of *his* best hopes and dreams. He sought his own reflection, one that, in his mirror, was omnipotent and perfect. Faults or flaws, as he perceived them, were anything from my need for eyeglasses at an early age to those 3 inches of grass that I would occasionally miss with the lawnmower.

I remember being summoned to the kitchen one night to be introduced to some new neighbors. I had on a T-shirt and brown horn-rimmed glasses. My father introduced me as his "four-eyed, frail son." He hated the fact that I wore glasses and that my arms protruded from my T-shirt like two thin pipes. I was so thin, in fact, that my father took me to a doctor and asked him, "Why is my son's chest concaved? It looks like a chicken breast! You can see his ribs." That country doctor had the rare gift of common sense. He said, "Don't worry about him. Feed him, and he will grow into his body." My father hated the fact that, as he saw it, I had a flaw in my design, and he reminded me of this at every turn.

Because of this, I would retreat into my own world, a world where imagination was put into play through sports and kids playing army. I may have been frail, but I threw myself into the fray. I broke those glasses a few times, and I taped them together with white tape. I turned inward from insecurity and would be deflated when I was reminded by my father of what I lacked.

My father's pronounced alcoholism distanced him more and more from active participation in the household. After school, I could spot him in the garage or passed out on the sofa. He began his day as I was ending mine. My mother was my only checkpoint, but she was busy with three other kids. She kept a tight rein on me, but when she wasn't looking, I took full advantage of those windows of freedom.

I was a rebellious teen, full of hormones and anger. I seethed in quiet desperation, detesting anything and anyone who would point out my shortcomings. My body began to develop, and I started to fill out those T-shirts. I grew my hair and snuck around the back of the house to smoke cigarettes at night. I would move with stealth into the kitchen and take a few beers with me. When questioned, I would pair my blank expression and open-palmed innocence with a look that said, "What? Me?"

In those days, I pushed against the envelope of rules—the boundaries that my siblings, out of respect or fear, never approached, let alone crossed. My recalcitrance became a major source of friction between my father and me, and it manifested itself through his baleful stare and caustic reproach. When the clock struck midnight, I was expected to be home—but what did I do? I stayed out until the roosters crowed, signaling the break of dawn. I was hanging out with other disenfranchised young adults, some of which my father had once put behind bars. We were rebels without a clue, and we reveled in our rebellion against authority.

On one typical night out (and typical always involved alcohol), as I approached my house after curfew, I could see the lights from the kitchen window in the distance. Cutting through the side lawn, I was about to make my usual planned entry, but this time, things didn't go as planned. My mother came running toward me through the grass in her red pajamas.

She was animated, her words punctuated by panicked gasps; I could barely comprehend what she was trying to say. My brother followed closely behind her, and almost in unison, they cried out, "Stop! Don't go in!" I asked my mom what was going on and went to the house anyway.

I looked inside, and there he was . . .

Now you need to know that my father had been retired for over three years by this point. When he turned in his badge, he locked away his revolver. It was a .38, and he was a crack shot. I watched him do things with that revolver that seemed like trick shooting! He could turn it upside down, roll a baseball away from him, and hit it three times. I am not using artistic license here either; I saw it!

So when I noticed that .38 lying between him and what remained of a bottle of Cutty Sark whiskey, I felt nothing but fear.

I backed away from the light and ran into the shadows. I ran and ran and kept on running through the outskirts of town and into the countryside. Fueled by adrenaline and cortisol, time seemed suspended with each step. I felt like I was floating forward in a surreal space, a displaced outcast without a home or any form of sanctuary from the storm.

I ran until my lungs hurt.

Out of breath, hands on my knees, I stared at the barren ground. I started to think. I thought about the advice my father had given that shaken, bruised, and fearful boy in the garage, "Son, you can keep running from the bully, but one day you will run out of room." Well, this was the day—a defining moment in my life. I was out of room, and I wasn't going to run anymore.

I was going to face this fear. I walked home, and I entered the front door quietly, crept up the stairs like a thief in my own house, and barricaded my bedroom door. That first step was the most crucial in my life, and it set the stage for everything that followed.

I used my father as an object lesson of what I did not want to become. I sympathized with his weakness, but I would not bend a knee to excuses, and I would never surrender to a condition that I could not control. I would see things as closely as I could for what they were, accept them, move through them, or try a new way to improve upon them. I would not confuse intimidation for strength or the belittlement of others for a relative feeling of superiority.

To quote C. S. Lewis, "You can't go back and change the beginning, but you can start where you are and change the ending." So I made an uneasy peace with my father. We often navigated separate spheres of the house. Neither one of us offered words of affection. However, in time, the caustic language and antagonistic behavior would subside.

Object Lessons

As I learned when it came to my father, the first step to freedom is to accept something for what it is, not reinvent it as something you want it to be. The next step is to forgive and, if possible, understand. I accepted my past for what it was; I forgave my father long ago for all that transpired under those low ceilings, and while I may never truly understand the source of his pain, I have moved far beyond the uncertainty and fear that marked my early life. I took these early experiences and used them as object lessons. Object lessons of what I did not want to become, and what I did not want to experience. I was ready to evolve to the next level, beyond the limits of uncertainty and fear. And if you are going to evolve and emerge as a better person, one willing and able to learn from failure, you're going to have to move beyond these limits as well.

The Blame Game

At some point in our lives, every one of us plays or has played the "blame game." As children, we learn to avoid unpleasant feelings by blaming others for our mistakes or missteps. It's deeply ingrained in us from our time on the playground. And because of its long-lasting roots, it's one of the biggest obstacles to success.

Blaming can be the metaphorical end of your journey to success. Blame is a fail-safe mechanism you use to say, "I wasn't the one who failed; it was a circumstance or something I couldn't control that caused the failure!" If you pass the baton to someone else, what's the purpose of continuing to run? You may not have reached the finish line, but hey, you did "your part." Passing the baton by blaming others is pointing the finger of failure at the external.

The need to blame others follows us into the workplace and into every corner of life. Accountability is a great buzzword as a concept, but it's really tough to practice on a consistent basis. It's tough because when we make a mistake or encounter failure, we don't want to expose ourselves as "less than"—as being deficient or incompetent.

Lose your excuses and do everything in your power to stop the blame game. Feel the power that comes from accepting personal ownership and exhibiting accountability for what you do and do not.

If you're going to own the successes, you have to own the failures. All too often, we choose to blame other people for the missteps and setbacks that we make in the attempt to achieve success. It's easy to point a finger, to blame others, the environment, or a condition for failure. What's often difficult is to assume personal responsibility for defeat. We revel in victories and wins, but we treat failure like a plague. However, growth comes from accepting responsibility for the setback while formulating a rational response to overcome those factors that prevented victory. While you're using logic to understand and dissect the nature and causes of failure, break your failures down into *major* versus *minor* failures. Once you stop blaming others and stop dispensing excuses, you'll find the reservoir of mental energy you need to get back in play and bring about a positive outcome.

Major Versus Minor Failures

Divide failures into two categories: major and minor. Quitting on your success is a major failure. It's a category of one. That's it. You're renouncing your responsibility to yourself to provide for a better station in life.

Everything else is a minor failure. Not only can you recover from a minor failure, but you already have done so a thousand times in your life. Whether it was attempting to walk, riding a bike, not getting a job, messing up a presentation, or failing a course, these are all things you can come back from.

Minor failures during the day have to be kept in perspective. Your goal is to improve every day, and you have to accept that minor failures are a part of that process. The long game is not the missteps you have during the hour, the day, or maybe even the month. Instead, it's the cumulative lessons you apply to realize your real goals.

You need to turn down the volume of day-to-day failures, and the only way I know to do this is to keep moving. *Momentum* is the blueprint for sustained success. Failure happens to each of us, but what we *do with it* makes the difference. If a failure doesn't result in you quitting, keep moving.

What Is It That You Really Want?

So how does this apply to your life? How does understanding, overcoming, and learning to embrace fear fit into the life you are living? You may not be Babe Ruth or Thomas Edison, but you *are* someone who picked up this book. You *are* someone who wants more success. You *are* someone who is looking to find a way through obstacles to create a better way of life for yourself. And you have the ability to make all of that a reality once you accept that failure is a part of life and a vehicle for positive progress.

Some people play small and safe; they succumb to fear and avoid risk. They never try to manage or overcome those obstacles that make them uncomfortable or those that could open them to the possibility of failure. They shrink the size of their lifestyle to fit the size of their paycheck. They don't do those things that would grow their income and provide enhanced lifestyle options. Too risky. After all, that would include discomfort and failure.

I've always thought that the purpose of life is to live your life to its most fulfilling promise. Purpose is your *why*. Purpose creates a passion that envelops, imbues, and creates the compelling *how* of what you do. To wake up every day with a chance to challenge and change, to improve and immerse yourself in the world. Unfortunately, some people don't want to be woken up. They want to stay in their cul-de-sac of safety, deep in the slumber of the comfortable and familiar. They will shut down when you mention the word "change." Because to change would mean they would have to look inside and do something that might bring a little pain. These people avoid pain first before they seek pleasure. They don't analyze gain; they seek to avoid pain, running all their life from change and uncertainty. By avoiding the pain of change, they don't grow, and they shrink into a box of self-constructed existence instead of choosing to create the vast enterprise that is life.

Getting up early, working late, and giving up weekends could be considered a sacrifice. So ask yourself what it is that you really want and what you are you willing to sacrifice to earn it. Once you have the answers, you'll have a guide, but you'll still be confronted daily with the fear of failure. Whether it's resistance, procrastination, or distraction, it will be there in disguise. Learn to say no to whatever it is—people, things, issues, or agendas—that derails or detracts you from doing whatever it is that brings you closer to what you must have. Learn the difference between what is important and what is urgent.

The Person You Could Become

What does learning the difference between being comfortable with what you have and knowing what you want look like? Take this scenario, for instance.

Every one of your days begins in a "cubicle." First, it's the box of your bedroom. Then you move from the bedroom to the kitchen and sit down at the table, pick up the remote, and turn on another box—the television. After watching Netflix, your favorite television series, or the news, you shower in a cubelike area and get into *another* box—your car, a bus, the metro.

On the way to work, you have your headphones on, zone out to music, or play a video game on your phone. *Thought* isn't a requisite because you've got your job down cold.

When you get to the office, you notice that guy again, the one who's always in here before anybody else. Why does he always have that "I'm going to make something happen today" look on his face? Then you notice the sleeves of your wrinkled shirt compared with his immaculate, custom-tailored suit. You also seem to be aware of the purpose in his pace as he enters his office—and it's not just any office; it's the corner office. You begin thinking, "Man, that guy started when I did. As a matter of fact, I went to a better school and had a better position when we started. What the heck happened?"

You're not being honest with yourself, are you? Are you someone who ever puts himself (or herself) out there? Do you only head to work to collect a check and go home and spend time with your friends on weekends? Are you doing everything but trying to create a career from your job?

Be honest with yourself. Have you created significance and value? Every day, you have the power to become better, or to be redundant and replaceable. When you push yourself to do more than just show up, you'll know you're in the right environment, one that promotes as a meritocracy. Once you find this place, you're going to be asked to do more things. These things will be new, and if you do them well, your performance will be rewarded with a promotion that you can use to turn your job into a career.

So what is it that's stopping you from pursuing your dream career, one that is full of goals that can lead to a better way of life for you and your loved ones? Is it lack of confidence? If so, then acquire the competence you need to be confident. Are you competent but not confident? If so, learn not to renounce your value as a person. Competency brings substance to confidence. Confidence comes from believing you have something important to say. If you have competence, you'll have something important to say, and it will move the meter on your career.

Back to our scenario:

You enter the break room, and there's the water-cooler crowd, a place where the disgruntled in the company congregate to gossip. Sometimes you're one of them. The guy in the tailored suit walks in, gets a cup of coffee, and walks out—acknowledging each in the room with a polite greeting. He doesn't linger. He moves on. He's moving his personal proposition forward, and he's about to engage in a risky venture that could generate more than your salary in income.

You think to yourself, "Screw this! I've had enough!" You straighten your tie and stand up a bit straighter, and you make a firm commitment to yourself. You're starting today.

You want a better way of life, and you understand that you're going to have to risk to gain. You're going to have to do what's uncomfortable, break out of the mindset that you earn a paycheck from a job, and start thinking that you can earn more income from a career. Your career is going to create more opportunities; you're going to position yourself to win by volunteering for tasks with a low possibility of failure. You're going to gain traction, and by volunteering, you're putting yourself in play for that promotion. Why? Because you're getting noticed! Some people fear the light of visibility. Seek it. Then you're going to raise the bar. You're going to ask for more. It will be a struggle, but you'll get it!

Align your actions with your agenda and your motives. If you want to get ahead, you're going to have to take risks. You want more, and to get more, you have to learn, fail, and grow. Sure it's a process that could result in failure, but remember this: All you need to do is to succeed once, and you'll be on your way! After all, that's the innovator's creed.

No more wasting time. Get in early; get engaged; do things that mean something. Don't just take on tasks to fill your day.

Your Obligation

Here is where your victory over fear comes into play. It will give you the opportunity to break out of your comfort zone, to learn new skills, to become indispensable. Now that you know how to manage your fear, to embrace it, to use it, you can finally become unstoppable.

In order to get what you want, you have to do those things that give you the confidence to do just a little bit more the next day. Yes, there is an element of risk, but the next day brings the new opportunity that you create, or one that you see, seize, and make available from your applied competence. Career development holds personal responsibility as a nonnegotiable trait. Making a better way in life for yourself and others is an obligation. Don't cede your power. Don't give it away so someone else can dictate your fate. Your power resides in your personal responsibility to learn more, do more, and become more.

Framing Failure

1. **Open the door to change.**

   People fear change and loss, but all progress is dependent upon your willingness to accept change and take intelligent risks to expand beyond your comfort zone. If you're going to achieve your goals, you're going to act in ways that are contrary to your brain's preference for safety. The more audacious the goal, the more likely the chance of failure. Get used to it—nothing worthy or of value was ever created without dissecting failure's lessons.

2. **Take a 3D look at the obstacle.**

   Take a step back from the fray and try to look at the obstacle in the most detached way possible. Is this a hill worth fighting for, or is this not worth expending the effort that you need to win the battle? Some positions are untenable—unwinnable situations where you're just swimming upstream, never making it to shore. Can you win? Can you succeed? Or is this the wrong hill?

   What do you need to learn? Who can help you? And what do you need to do to move through or around the obstacle? Take action now—start learning; recruit your allies; get moving!

3. **Denial of an obstacle doesn't remove it.**

   Sooner or later you'll have to deal with the obstacle that's preventing your success. When you deny its existence, you only delay its presence. Dispense with it now; don't let it fester. Things often get more difficult in time, not easier.

CHAPTER 5

Become a
Master of Failure

*Something experts in all fields tend to do
when they're practicing is to operate outside
of their comfort zone and study themselves
failing. The best figure skaters in the world
spend more of their practicing time practicing
jumps that don't land than lesser figure skaters
do. The same is true of musicians. When
most musicians sit down to practice, they
play the parts of pieces they're good at. Of
course they do; it's fun to succeed! But expert
musicians tend to focus on the parts that are
hard. The parts they haven't yet mastered.
The way to get better at a skill is to force
yourself to practice just beyond your limits.*

—JOSHUA FOER, *MOONWALKING WITH EINSTEIN*

Adam Kreek is a two-time rowing Olympian with a degree in geotechnical engineering and hydrology from Stanford University. Rowing is a mentally and physically demanding sport that revolves around the fact that the sum is greater than the individual parts. It's a team sport, but every person in the boat has to not only work together, but do the work alone at the same time.

Kreek is a professional speaker today, and he shares his story of happiness despite failure. In Kreek's words, "There is an incredible power that is unleashed when you don't quite get what you want yet you find a way to remain happy."

When you invest and extend as much time and effort as Kreek did in pursuit of his sport's ultimate goal, an Olympic gold, one would think that there's not much room for philosophical contemplation. But Kreek is a different breed. He espouses the philosophy that if we "fail happily and we fail effectively, we gain more self-confidence. We can have greater self-esteem. We have more connection to each other, to the universe. In fact, we become more successful."

The joy for Kreek is in the striving, the camaraderie, and the process of becoming more. He doesn't tie his emotional well-being to the outcome. Instead, it's the constant quest for improvement that not only gives him purpose, but also lights the fire that fuels his desire to achieve more.

Kreek informs his audiences that the most important thing he learned at the Olympics was a lesson on failure.

Kreek was the fastest starboard on the team until he says a "big, bald, Viking-looking guy named Jake Wetzel" started to kick his butt. Life presents each of us with our own competitive arena. At the Olympic level, the intensity of the competition is ratcheted up to its highest degree. Competition brings out the best and the worst in our nature, and

Kreek was no exception to this rule. He didn't like being displaced as the fastest. His ego was dented, and he immediately thought Wetzel to be an idiot and someone he wanted to physically harm.

Emotion was creating a distance between teammates who, theoretically, shared a common goal. Kreek stepped back from the emotional sway and reverted to the logic that served him well at Stanford: "Wait a minute—here we are competing against each other, but we're on the same team. Maybe I can learn from him."

I remember giving a sales talk once, and after my 60-minute keynote, I asked a question: "Who's the top salesperson in this company?" After a moment of silence in a room of 400 people, fingers pointed at a woman in the back of the room. I asked, "How many of you walked into her office and asked her for advice? She's number one for a reason." Haltingly, four hands went up. Then I asked, "Now who's asked to take her to lunch?" No hands went up. Don't be one of those people. Start to realize that teachers are in your midst. Maybe you're too proud to ask, but more often than not, the person with the knowledge or skill you want to learn is more than happy to share it.

Serving as testimony, Kreek's story continues:

One day Kreek approached Wetzel and asked him to have lunch. As they sat in front of a pile of bagels and a dozen eggs, Kreek asked Wetzel point-blank, "Jake, what's your secret to success? How are you so successful?"

Kreek didn't expect the answer Wetzel gave him. "I seek failure." Kreek was in shock and asked Wetzel if he was putting him on.

Wetzel went on to explain a Monday-through-Saturday step-by-step approach. He explained that he would pick one workout every week and train to his current limit, that boundary right before failure. In his words, "I willingly push myself through my known limit, and know I will embrace failure. My body will fail on me and for the rest of the week as well. I will know what my limit is, and I will hover below it, and in fact, the greatest point of growth occurs right below your limit."

The lightbulb went on. Kreek found the brilliance in the method and embraced it as a way of consistent improvement. It became his edge. He embraced the process, method, and importance of failure, and it made all the difference. His team later won the gold medal at the 2008 Summer Olympics in Beijing.

Be one of those people who work right up to their edge of comfort. You don't have to be an Olympian or a professional athlete to know the value in the mindset that drives this behavior. The key is to feel uncomfortable and embrace the pain, then push a little more every week. Like Kreek and Wetzel, seek failure from the uncomfortable. When you find its sweet spot, you will have what it takes to get to the next level. You'll be armed with resilience, resolve, and a feeling of achievement—and you'll need all three to become a next-level performer.

Use All Emotions as a Tool—
Even the Negative Ones

To fail forward, you have to distance yourself from emotions. You're only human—you will feel emotions first—but you need to react strategically, not emotionally. Feel your emotions, move beyond them, and start using logic instead of feeling.

In order to shift from emotions to strategic thought, you must attempt first to limit and then to stop the failure loop that often plays doom and gloom in your head. Own your mistakes, but know the distinction between your self-worth and failure as a condition or event. You are not a failure, and don't ever let yourself think of failure as being synonymous with you. Next you have to move out of the emotional space and start thinking rationally. Logic will be your guide to dispassionately analyze what went wrong. Then, armed with real data, you can make the adaptations necessary to improve the outcome on the next try.

Resilience

A user-friendly definition of resilience is a "bend but do not break" mentality. It's like a muscle, and using it will help to develop it. While resilience may not come easy for everyone, you can develop a stronger bounce-back muscle with practice in the form of failure.

Research on resilience as a determinate of future success can be traced to the work of Stanford researcher Carol

Dweck. Her groundbreaking book *Mindset* differentiates those who have a fixed mindset from those with a growth mindset. A growth mindset isn't fixated on a grade or result, but rather the process and the enjoyment of trying to solve seemingly insoluble problems. A fixed mindset is one that holds intelligence as innate and unable to be altered or changed. Not surprisingly, those with a fixed mindset are grade-oriented.

The defining point in Dweck's career arc began in 1998 when she conducted a study of 400 fifth graders. The study involved problem-solving tests to see how they coped with adversity and challenge.

She gave each student a series of simple puzzles. After they completed the puzzles, each of the students was given his or her score. The students were also given something else—verbal praise. Half of the students were lauded for their intellect: "You must be smart at this." The other half received praise for their focused effort: "You must've worked really hard."

Dweck was testing for the potential effect that these rather mundane sentences could have on the students' mindsets. She wanted to find out if those two sentences could influence the students' attitude toward success and failure; if the sentences could have a measurable impact on the students' persistence and performance. The results were quite telling.

When they completed the initial test, the students were offered a choice between taking a difficult or easy test. Two-thirds of those students who received praise for their intellect selected the easier test. Those students who chose the easy test didn't want to risk losing their "smart" label by subjecting themselves to failure in the form of the harder test. Conversely, 90 percent of those students praised for effort raised their hands for the tough test. These students weren't as in invested in success as they were in the exploration of a rewarding challenge. For them, it was about proving just how much effort they were willing to expend to get that bounce of accomplishment from the work.

Then Dweck raised the bar! Each student was given a test so difficult that it was impossible for any of them to succeed. Dweck found a striking difference between the ways praise-oriented and effort-oriented students responded to failure. Those who received recognition for their intelligence construed their failures as valid proof that they just weren't good at puzzles. On the other hand, the effort-praised group stayed with the test, persevering much longer and enjoying the process much more than the intelligence-praised group. More important, they didn't suffer a lack of confidence. Then Dweck closed out the experiment by doling out tests of equal difficulty to the first test the students took.

The results? The performance of those praised for intelligence declined by 20 percent compared with the first test, even though the difficulty level was similar. This decline is in sharp contrast to the 30 percent increase in test scores produced by the effort-praised group. *Failure* actually motivated them. Dweck was stunned that the difference between the two groups could be found in the students' interpretation of those few words that were spoken after the initial test.

"Mindsets frame the running account that's taking place in people's heads," Dweck writes. "They guide the whole interpretation process." To summarize her findings:

- Praise effort, not talent.
- Endeavor to transform abilities through consistent applied effort.
- Shift your mindset to interpret challenges as *real* learning opportunities, rather than *potential* threats.
- Understand that failure isn't a personal indictment of innate gifts, but rather an opportunity for your continued improvement.

Fixed Versus Growth Mindset

In this study, the students with a fixed mindset felt the sting of failure. From their fixed-mindset perspective, their intelligence was on trial, and they failed. As Dweck puts it, "Instead of luxuriating in the power of 'yet,' they were gripped in the tyranny of 'now.'" Perhaps this doesn't come as a shock, but the ones with a fixed mindset told the researchers they'd probably cheat instead of studying more if they failed. Another group said they would find other people who didn't do as well, and using a relative standard of comparison, they would feel better because they weren't alone.

The fixed-mindset students ran from potential danger, otherwise known as error. On the other hand, the growth-mindset students were engaged. In electrical tests, their brains showed high activity levels, and the brains of those with a fixed mindset showed none.

This resulted in Dweck asking fundamental questions: "How are we raising our children? For now or for yet? Are we raising kids to get the A in order to get into a good school, get a good job, and then what? They haven't learned to fail. They need validation based on a result, and that will dictate the rest of their lives."

Dweck works with employers who seek her out, and she explains that "we have already raised a generation of young workers who can't get through the day without an award." Dweck believes in praising wisely. But instead of praising intelligence or talent, she praises the process that the kids are engaged in, as well as the effort, strategies, and will-power that drive their improvement.

Dweck calls willpower "the great equalizer" and believes that this trait is a better indicator of future success, even over IQ.

But what about confidence? Dweck has found that using the words "not yet" gave kids greater confidence and encouraged them to create a path forward from persistence. The children from the study could move beyond their comfort zone, learn something new, and allow their neurons in the brain to form "new, stronger connections" and, over time, get smarter.

Learning to Admit
When You're Wrong

As you shift from emotional feeling to strategic thinking, focus on the facts. Facts can offer a rational perspective, whereas feelings cloud logic.

If your previous way of thinking resulted in a setback, you'll be destined to repeat it unless you figure out why you failed. You might need to solicit help to sort it out in the form of a "sounding board" who can offer an unbiased assessment of your failure. Even with the best intent and painstaking analysis of the data, you can still fall prey to the human condition of blind spots.

For me, until I brought in outside help from a consultant, I was stuck in my original way of thinking. In this instance, my pride was wounded from the embarrassment of failure. I just couldn't figure out what went wrong. I was too close to the process, and I was emotional. With my ego in my pocket, I called a consultant from Texas and invited him in to generate the type of information that would provoke the conversation necessary to produce my "Eureka!" moment.

Failure can make you spin out of control and blame yourself for an outcome you couldn't control. Mastering your emotions is essential if you are to master failure as a tool that forges success.

Let's look at some specific ways you can master your emotions by working through negative feelings:

1. **PROCESS YOUR FEELINGS KEEPING A JOURNAL.** This will help you articulate your emotions and stop you from lashing out.

2. **TRY TO CONNECT THE DOTS.** Write down everything that happened and reflect on it—what led to the failure? Stick only to the facts.

3. **CHOOSE YOUR COUNSEL WISELY.** Find someone whose advice you value. Feedback is crucial. Truth and support will buoy you and give you that lift you might need. Mentors, close colleagues from outside your company, or professional consultants will help to provide the feedback necessary to adjust your means and methods.

4. **KEEP YOUR MAIN GOAL AT THE FOREFRONT OF YOUR THOUGHTS.** Ask yourself, "Is my goal still realistic and still attainable?" Now take a look at your subgoals and ask yourself, "Are they the best indicators of incremental success?" Adjust as necessary and realize that your subgoals may need to be adjusted first.

Get Out of Your Failure Loop

Dwelling on the negative can create a self-fulfilling prophecy of despair and defeat. You're already beaten before you start if all you can think about is a negative outcome. While it's important to think about as many things as you can that could go wrong, the reason for thinking about them in the first place is to find creative ways to prevent them. When you focus on the negatives, your thinking renounces the possibility of a positive outcome. You lose the power of positivity. Positivity isn't ignoring or failing to consider the negative. Rather, it's a mindset that is oriented toward making things happen for you, not to you.

Often we look in the past and think about those failures that we've already endured. We've endured them, but we haven't learned from them. And we're condemned to repeat them if we don't extract and apply the lessons from the experience. How many people have failed to try because they're stuck in a "failure loop," replaying past events that now appear to be real? If you don't dispatch the past for what it is, a place to learn and grow from, you're going to be stuck in the memories that keep you confined in its prison of self-constructed misery.

Getting out of a failure loop is emotional. When you're upset, you're at the very bottom of your brain. Emotion is clouding your ability to think rationally. Time to hit the reset button. Here's how:

1. TAKE A DEEP BREATH. I know this may sound simple, but before you do anything else, take a step back and breathe deeply. Only when you start to slow down will your emotions start to quiet. Focusing on your breathing will help you to get out of the instinct part of your brain (the bottom) and into the rational part of your brain (the top).

2. FEEL YOUR EMOTIONS; THEN CHECK THEM. After giving your feelings a little space for acknowledgment, it's time to let them go, to make the switch to strategic thinking. In order to do that, you need to be in the rational part of your brain, not stuck at the lower end with emotions.

Start to take yourself away from feeling and toward thinking. Break the emotional ties of feeling like a failure. Get out of this pattern of thinking. Ask yourself: "What is really happening here? How would I rather feel?" These cues will aid you in making the transition. Forgive yourself and forgive everyone involved.

3. **CREATE AN OBJECTIVE FRAMEWORK.** It's important to evaluate the failure dispassionately. Take a step back and look at all parts of the equation. Look and see: What kept you from your goal? What steps can you take to avoid the pattern of failure? From there, each specific failure will provide you with an opportunity to improve by giving you clues on how not to fail. Start to read those clues and spot patterns. This will get easier over time.

4. **TEST-DRIVE YOUR NEW DIRECTION.** Once the clouds are cleared, you can start to see the answers. How can you move forward? What new steps do you need to take? What old ones do you need to abandon? Be specific and intentional about your goals, and visualize yourself making them a reality. Picture yourself step-by-step. Then make a promise to yourself to not revert to old ways just because they are familiar.

5. **ASSIGN A VALUE TO FAILURE.** Now that you see the results evolving, you will start to value failure as the tool it can be. Continue to be vigilant for signs of failure, and start tweaking your direction along the way. Try not to pause, as this can cause you to fret and return you to an emotional response. If you focus on your new steps, you'll begin to see new results. They in themselves will

be encouraging. If some are not yielding the anticipated success at the rate you anticipated, revise them.

6. **CREATE YOUR SUCCESS PROFILE.** This may sound basic, but once you've figured out what works, get out your journal and make detailed notes. Write down everything that brought you closer to a successful outcome. You can refer to this "success profile" to avoid slipping back to the old ways and the ineffective methods that failed to produce a successful result. As you build your profile, you will find an armory of successful strategies and tactics to draw from as you surge toward your next victory.

7. **BE GRATEFUL.** Make it a point to practice gratitude for opportunities that come your way. Even in failure you can find an opportunity to give thanks. Sure, failure is a powerful punch in the gut, but it is not as painful as the sting of regret. Having the opportunity to change and move forward is something to be thankful for.

You might have to go back and repeat some steps in this process if you feel you are not moving forward or if you sense that even your new steps aren't working for you. Remember to think of these steps as a loop. Here are the ABCs of the process to use as a simple memory tool to keep you moving through the loop:

- *A*djust, *a*dapt, and generate *a*ctivity toward your goal. Take time to reflect; then get back in the game. Adjust and adapt according to what you have learned from your setback, and determine your next activity to move forward in the process.

- *B*lock out the noise from the naysayers who say you won't succeed and the voice inside that says you can't.
- Have clarity and confidence. You have to see with clarity what you want, and you have to have confidence in your ability to get it.

Master Your Mind

Now that you've mastered your emotions, it's time to master your mind. The sooner you do this, the faster you'll be able to work through your emotions the next time you fail. It's easy to get overwhelmed by failure, but at the same time, you can become overconfident from positive change and success. Think about what you've learned from your past failure, and remember that blame and justification will bog you down. You need to take personal responsibility and move forward:

- Consider if you need to overhaul your system of thought or simply make minor adjustments.
- Plan your approach, organize the material you need to begin, and, on the fly, continue to refine your system to improve your product. This is how you position yourself to win.
- Use your mentors and peers to help you analyze your system and approach. Look for the weak links in your strategy and methods. You will find them. Once you have, address them.

Framing Failure

1. **Seek failure.**

   Learn, as Wetzel did, that growth demands you push yourself just a little beyond your reach every day. He set himself up for failure by design. He knew that if his efforts were just beyond his ability to effectively meet his goal, he would come back with better effort and extended reach the next day.

2. **Not all failures are created equal.**

   Break failure down into two categories: acceptable and unacceptable. Acceptable failures are those minifailures that are not life-threatening; they won't take you out of the game completely if you fail. Megafailures are death and injury—things that physically harm you and take you out of the game.

3. **Develop a failure threshold.**

   You have to create your own tolerance-to-risk guideline. You've got to weigh your gain against your potential loss.

4. **Practice, practice, practice!**

   Deliberate practice and the adherence to rituals is the requisite sacrifice that mastery requires. Practice is more than intermittent exercise; it's the habitual discipline to improve.

5. **The best product, presentation, or process is one that is crafted from mastery.**

   Deliberate practice is transformational. Perspective is your weapon of understanding. Take the long view:

94

Understand that acceptable failures may occur during the day, month, or year, but if you're learning from failure, they're necessary to have a rewarding life.

CHAPTER 6

It's Goal Time

Define and Plan for Success

Most great people have attained their greatest
success just one step beyond their greatest failure.

—NAPOLEON HILL

Rome wasn't built in a day, and neither is success. Great accomplishments take time. Mastering a craft, acquiring a skill, and adopting disciplined habits take consistent effort and dedication.

Whether your "big goal" is crafting your next masterpiece, planning your ascent to the Oval Office, or positioning yourself for your next raise, focus on the fundamentals that make your big goal a reality. You must build your empire just like the Romans, stone by stone.

The laying of stones embodies a process. It's a systematic approach that is subject to disciplined habit, resolve, patience, and retrospection. Success and failure don't happen overnight—both are the product of small, often mundane daily wins and losses. It's continuous immersion in day-to-day struggles through detours, distractions, and obstacles.

Experts define goal setting as the selection of a target or objective you intend to achieve. Rather than asking yourself what it is you want to achieve, ask yourself what it is you can endure to achieve it. What kind of pain threshold can you tolerate in pursuit of your goal? Setting goals is easy; realizing them takes work, pain, and sacrifice. Start here. Ask yourself the question, "What is it that I'm willing to endure to achieve my goal?"

Whatever your goal, there will be trade-offs that accompany them. Every Olympian wants a gold medal, but few of us are willing to train like an Olympian. Goal setting then is not just about the rewards of the good life. It's also about the costs you're willing to pay to live that life.

The cost each of us must pay to enjoy the fruits of a better life is the pain of failure. Failure is accompanied by the sting of rejection, the feeling of shame, and the bitter taste of disappointment. The most significant advantage that failure provides resides in the lessons it doles out in the process. These lessons will shorten the distance between where you are now and where you intend to go, while lessening the pain of the next experience.

The first lesson you can learn from failure is to avoid setting yourself up for it. As we learned from Andy Stumpf, the totality of an event or goal can be overwhelming. While you need crystal clarity about the nature of your goal, you need to break down the small steps you have to take to achieve it. (Remember, you need to "make it to the next meal.")

As audacious as your goal may be (and I'm a fan of *big*, obnoxious goals!), you have to set realistic objectives to cash the obscene checks that your mind writes. Your goals aren't limited to monetary gain. There are physical, emotional, and spiritual goals as well as those financial milestones that make for a life.

So think of how much better you would be—physically, mentally, emotionally, and spiritually—if every day you thought about and then acted on one thing that would contribute to your improvement. We can go to our graves with the best intention, the unmet potential that will expire with us if we don't pay attention to those small things now. Fundamentals will keep you on track. If you ignore the basics, you'll leave your success to luck and chance, hoping and wishing that things happen for you.

If you are to approximate your potential, you have to start and stick with fundamentals. The "better you" begins in the planning stages. Once the planning is complete and it's time to implement the plan, focus on fundamentals. You'll find that adherence to fundamentals will be integral to your continued development.

It's time for you to build your success (to reach your goal), much like building Rome, stone by stone. The stones are the fundamental foundation for your success framework.

Stage 1: Play It Forward by Looking Back

Think about your time of demise. You're on your deathbed reflecting on your life. Do you have regret? What would you have become if you had no self-imposed limits?

Take the limits down, let your imagination run wild, and describe what that reality would have looked like:

....

....

....

....

....

....

....

Stage 2: Get Specific with Your Goals

In this section, create a "to-do" list that supports the goals drafted in Stage 1. For example, if you want to run a full marathon (26.219 miles), what do you need to do first? From the shoes you buy, to the partner you run with, to the pace you run at, you need to work up to a 5K, a 10K, and a half marathon before striking out for your big goal, the full marathon. Use the same principle in your financial endeavors. If you want to be a millionaire, you first have to find your way to the $100K in personal income. How do you get there? What do you need to do? Who around you is doing it now? And who has done it?

....

....

....

....

....

....

....

Stage 3: Limit Competing Distractions

When you have too many goals, you have no goal. What you have is a bunch of objectives, wishes, or wants, but not a real "dig in, do what it takes, make it happen" goal. Competing goals look like this: "I want to be the star sales-person in my company, but I also want to be a triathlete. And, oh, by the way, I think a gourmet chef sounds good, too!" Time, energy, and focus are vital in the pursuit of what you deem to be most important. You need to establish one major goal and separate that goal from all the other hobbies that seem like a goal.

Have you ever seen people chase so many things, they end up going in circles and don't even accomplish one of those things? They run out of energy. They run out of time. And they run out of the willpower it takes to crush that one, big audacious goal. Chasing too many goals is a design for failure. Taking the time to know what you truly want while making the commitment to do what it takes to get it will start you on the path to fulfillment.

What are your competing distractions, and what do you need to do to limit them?

Stage 4: Identify Who, What, When, and Where

Who are those people who can help you achieve your goal? What can they contribute? When can they begin their contribution? And where do they begin?

....

....

....

....

....

....

....

Stage 5: Keep Track of Your Progress

Start a success journal. Create two columns: one column for those accomplishments that brought you closer to your goal, and another column for those distractions that impeded you from the tasks you needed to complete to make your day a success. Look for the lessons in your past successes and failures. What worked and why? What obstacles stopped you and why? This is where honesty provides direction. If you're willing to learn from both columns, you have what it takes to make that progressive journey forward.

You may or may not be surprised by the amount of time wasters that litter your day—trading idle gossip, engaging in tasks that are comfortable but useless, and not doing the tough stuff that success demands.

Don't fly blind—measure your progress. Say you're in a business that demands that you meet your quota every quarter. History proves that if you make 100 calls a day and generate 3 appointments (one of which you close), you make your quota. But quota is for average, and who wants to be average? If your personal goal is wealth creation, then you need to make far more than the mandated average of 100 calls a day. In fact, you need to blow that number up and dial until your fingers bleed if you want to generate forward thrust. Measure the difference between how many appointments you set from 100 calls a day and how many you can set from 300 a day. The feedback you receive from this form of measurement will provide you with the way to blow up average and cash more checks as you earn enhanced lifestyle options. Without measurement and the willingness to be held to your own personal standard of improvement, backslide will occur in a short period of time.

Create Your Own Definition of Success

My mindset is firmly entrenched in Earl Nightingale's belief, "All success begins by serving others." And he offered what I believe is one of the most succinct and powerful definitions of success: "Success is really nothing more than the progressive realization of a worthy ideal."

Let's examine the most important words in the sentence: "progressive," "realization," and "worthy." Progress demands risk, and it is accompanied by failure. That's evolution. Survival of the species was predicated on those who could adapt. Adaptation had many failures, and this is the nature of life.

Success isn't found in a suit and tie or in a position, title, or measurement of economic scale. How would I define success? I came up with "Success is the realization of my own expectation." It is my own definition, and to this day, it challenges me to create higher-level expectations and do what it takes to realize them.

It's critical to define success in your own terms *before* embarking on a new endeavor because it's more than a mantra; it's a "North Star" during your journey to achievement. When I find myself completely turned around after spiraling through failure, I can look to my definition of success: "The realization of my own expectation." I can then ask myself, "Did I meet my expectations by dedicating 100 percent of my focus, energy, and resources to this goal?" Since the answer is no, I can reflect on the steps I had taken up until this point, identify where I went wrong, make the necessary changes to my approach, and move forward. Remember, failure is only failure if you refuse to learn from it.

To articulate *your* definition of success, answer these two questions with four, five, six words or short phrases:

1. What am I passionate about?

....

....

....

....

....

....

....

....

2. What are my gifts? (Modesty is banned! What are you truly talented at?)

For example, Maddie is passionate about outreach, connection, and relationship building. Her gifts are communicating with people, engaging people, and persuading them. So for Maddie, success is "to inspire transformation in my community through my writing."

....

....

....

....

....

....

....

....

When you learn to define success in your terms, you can then create the goals that are consistent with your definition. This will also help you establish a clarity in your goal and a direction in which to achieve it.

Look in the Mirror

Ask yourself these questions: "Do I have the right frame of mind to do what I have to do? Can I learn the skills to do it? And is this the right place to spend my time doing it?" For instance, no matter how much I wanted to be an astronaut, I couldn't. I couldn't get through introductory calculus, let alone understand anything in the realm of physics. My astronaut career would've failed to launch from day one. Now I could have a great attitude, I could show up early, and people could try to teach me, but no, I couldn't be an astronaut.

Are you one of those people that show up every day, ready to influence your life from the terms you dictate? Are you prepared to take it to the next level, determined to change the game? Are you always learning, curious for what's next, finding the courage to apply what you've learned and realizing that failure isn't fatal and that success, as Churchill said, isn't final?

Framing Failure

1. **Be clear about what it is you must have.**

   Sometimes goals get too fuzzy. You can begin to feel frustrated when you don't see an end to your effort. Look back on where you have stumbled at this in the past and honestly think about where you made mistakes. Did you take on too much? Did you rely on others? Did you not have all the information you needed to proceed? Turning your goal into a reality is a progressive journey through hard work, failure, adaptation, and victory. But first you have to know where you've been and where you're going!

2. **Perfect is the enemy of good.**

   Don't compare yourself to others, and stop trying to be perfect. Both are zero-sum games. There's always someone with more, and perfect is an illusion. Your goals are *your* goals. Don't be so hard on yourself. Write out a permission slip, "It's okay to screw up," and keep it close at hand! Stay in touch with your goals, but understand that to achieve them, you're going to take a few falls and make some missteps—it's okay.

3. **Innovate, iterate, incorporate.**

   James Dyson famously developed more than 5,000 prototypes before he hit it big with his bagless vacuum.

(Now, there's your baseline!) Innovation is the product of failure. It's the process of trial and error that makes success possible. You try, fail, and make changes that you incorporate, evaluate, and modify if you don't get the result you intend. It will be rare that you get it right the first time. Improvement is about perseverance, patience, and discipline. Keep your eye on the goal but stay in your laboratory of innovation until what you incorporate brings success.

4. **Remember that aiming high is a great aspiration, but missing the target leads to frustration.**

Try making your subgoals possible, not impossible, to reach. The confidence and the reward gained from achieving one subgoal will build upon the next subgoal. Keep moving your subgoals in incremental steps toward your big goal.

5. **Think about your life—strive for incremental improvement.**

Try to make yourself just a little bit better every day. If you do this, in time, your skills and confidence will compound. Every day, just a little bit of improvement, and you'll become unstoppable. The key is to hold your ground, make the change, see the improvement, and then don't backtrack. Next, next, next.

CHAPTER 7

The Road to Success

Never confuse a single defeat
with a final defeat.
—F. SCOTT FITZGERALD

The Long and Winding Road

Your road to success is a process and a journey, not a destination. You can't pause along the road and hope improvement will ensue from lack of activity—success is always under construction.

The author Stephen King's road to success was anything but a straight line. As a matter of fact, his story is one of self-belief, perseverance, and talent. Self-confidence is essential, and your willingness to engage in intentional practice is a prerequisite for success, but the ability to learn from failure is the great differentiator between those who move forward on their current road to success and those who need to find a new path.

King wrote constantly and was rewarded with rejection slips after each submission to Alfred Hitchcock's

Mystery Magazine. As King recalls, "Each slip bore Alfred Hitchcock's unmistakable profile in red ink, and wished me good luck with my story." Over time, King started to make a game out of the rejection. Instead of throwing the slips out, he nailed them in a stack to his bedroom wall. Imagine going to sleep at night, looking at rejection, and waking up, only to face it the next day.

The rejection slips continued piling up, and soon the nail wasn't big enough to hold all the letters. So he got a bigger spike and kept on writing. In a capsule, this is the essence of *Fail More.* Rejection will slap you in the face, not once, not twice, but so many times that you'll lose count. But like King, your purpose will compel you to keep going, adapt, and grow.

After myriad impersonal rejections, King found hope in the one personalized response he received after eight years of failed submissions. Even though his manuscript was rejected, he found hope in the unsigned message that read, "Don't staple manuscripts, loose pages + paper clip = correct way to submit copy." Although it was cold water to the face, King did find it useful. Often in the midst of failure, there is that ray of light that, however dimly, provides direction. For King, he started to use the advice of "loose pages + paper clip = correct way to submit copy" on every manuscript going forward. He also thought, "Finally, someone is paying attention to me." Even though the rejections kept coming, King was progressing, getting better and better. He was steadfast in his resolve to be published. His persistence would pay off again, when one of the magazines wrote back, "Your stuff is good, but it's not for us: Keep submitting."

Although it may be hard to believe the rejection that the talent that is Stephen King endured at this level, he did what you must do with your gifts. We all start at a place where we need to improve if we are going to succeed on a more significant scale. Once you reach the next level of success, the one that you scratched, clawed, and fought for, through tears, through rejection, and through emotional pain, you have to raise the bar to the next level if you are to yet again achieve more significant success. He was persistent, and you must be too. He followed his purpose, and so must you.

King viewed rejection as a learning process, and he stayed with the process until he began learning, improving, and finally getting published.

We All Need Our Champions

When King wrote *Carrie*, he didn't like it. The story felt foreign to him. He had difficulty getting inside the head or even caring about the emotions of a teenage girl. He didn't think it was the best material he had written to date, so he tossed it in the wastebasket. It could have ended there, but it didn't. King's biggest, loudest champion—his wife—pulled the manuscript out of the trash, read it, and encouraged him to finish it. She was intrigued and wanted to know how it would end!

King told her he didn't know "jack shit" about high school girls, but his wife said she would help him. She thought her husband had something with *Carrie*. As King recalls, "Sometimes you have to keep going, even when you don't feel like it. And sometimes when you're doing good work, it doesn't feel like it. But you have to do the work."

113

King, who was a professor at a local college, wound up working on *Carrie* between classes. After making some changes and finishing the manuscript, he sent it off to the publisher, Doubleday. King was in the teacher's room grading papers when the intercom came on and the voice on the other end asked if King was available for a phone call. He hurried down the hall, sensing a worst-case emergency. It was his wife on the other line—she was out of breath as she read a telegram from Bill Thompson from Doubleday which read, "CONGRATULATIONS. CARRIE OFFICIALLY A DOUBLEDAY BOOK. IS $2,500 ADVANCE OKAY? THE FUTURE LIES AHEAD. LOVE, BILL." An advance of $2,500 was a small amount, but King didn't know that, and he didn't have a literary agent to help him know it.

Not long after that call, he got another one. It was a Sunday, and King was alone in his apartment. His wife had taken the kids to her mother's for a visit, and he was working away on a new book. The phone rang. It was his contact at Doubleday, who asked, "Are you sitting down?"

King replied, "No, do I need to be?" He did, because moments later he was told that the paperback rights to Carrie were sold for $400,000.

And the rest is still being written . . .

Channeling Your Inner Stephen King

- *Your* goal needs to be clear and present, focused to the extreme. *You* must never lose sight of it. *King* found his purpose early. He loved to write; he wanted to be published, and nothing would stop that from becoming a reality.

- *King* engaged in that intentional practice that leads to mastery. Are *you* ready to enter the 10,000 hours+ of practice that mastery requires? There are no overnight successes—*King* proves this point. *You've* got to do the work.

- Do *you* have what it takes to be rejection-proof? Do *you* understand that rejection is a prerequisite for success? Accept that immediately, and get used to it! *King* didn't take rejection personally—he made it into a game. The more rejection he received, the more he was determined to improve his craft.

- Self-doubt and lack of confidence will derail you. No one will believe in you unless you first believe in yourself. Grow your confidence with small steps, little things that give you the impetus to try more. Don't run from rejection; use it as fuel. At first, *King* didn't believe in *Carrie*, but he never stopped believing in himself.

- Surround yourself with people who offer moral and intellectual support and feedback. You need assistance to become successful in life; you can't do it all alone. *King* had a major advocate. His wife believed in him, supported him, and encouraged him to keep going when he thought *Carrie* was a failure—and we should all be thankful she did.

Framing a Mental Picture

The road to success begins with your dreams. If you dared to dream in bold, living color, what would all-encompassing happiness feel like to you? Visualize it; then connect your feeling to your vision. Vision may be steeped in idealism, but for it to become reality, you must believe in the possibility of its achievement. Don't minimize your dreams; maximize them. Keep them big and bold. You need to create a deep impression of your goal and fix the image in your mind. Let it burn deeply into the recesses of your mind; keep it present and make it clear. Every day, hold that image and then picture the steps you need to take, the tasks you need to complete, and the people you need to meet, to make your vision a reality. You see, each step forward is progress if it is in alignment with your vision.

Remember to focus on your subgoals, those little achievements that move you closer to the realization of your big dream. Here's a dream-enabling caveat: Nothing happens unless you're willing to go all out and work for it.

There are a lot of blogs, books, articles, and podcasts that promise more with less. Better results, less work. Have you ever looked into the background of those who promise the goods without the work? I mean, what did they do, besides provide you with a shortcut around the road to success that doesn't include the heavy lifting of work?

An Instagram Influencer can post inspiring platitudes, but when that "feel good" wears off, it's your responsibility to light your own fire of motivation. No one can give you inspiration; it comes from a place deep inside you. Find your inspiration and visualize its inception.

The founder of McDonald's, Ray Kroc, provides a witty, yet accurate, assessment of instant success when he said, "I was an overnight success all right, but 30 years is a long, long night." You have to roll up your sleeves and do the work. You're going to break some nails, use pencils until they're stubs, and maybe destroy a laptop or two, but the assiduous application of focused effort toward an intended result is work.

The need to work doesn't go away. It's there every day. Either you're working in a progressive, meaningful fashion, or you're searching for shortcuts, a quick answer, or a panacea for success that is more illusion than reality. You are surrounded and bombarded by *talkers*—they haven't *done* anything, but they're preaching success as they try to get you to buy their message while distracting you from doing due diligence on the messenger. Our modern-day charlatans come at you from various social media platforms. How do you discover which people are real and which are getting out of someone's borrowed Lamborghini, yacht, or home, showing you the car, boat, or mansion they want you to believe they worked for? It's not theirs. It's a facade. People can't take away the work that you do—it's yours. Your product, your effort. Use caution when you believe something at face value from someone you don't know, whose only credibility and calling card is the material.

Images of the material goods you strive to obtain can provide a form of motivation, but *only* if you're willing to work for those goods. And I mean *real* work. Real work isn't the "upload" button. It's creating value for others as you build value for yourself. It's meeting with people, cultivating relationships, moving the needle from "job" to "career" and "career" to "legacy." Your goal has to be personalized. You have to own it. It has to come from your mind. It has to come from your motivation. It doesn't come from the motivation of others. The first step toward achieving your goal is to fix it in your mind and visualize the steps in detail that it takes to realize it.

Some scoff at the power of visualization; they think it's the stuff of wish, hope, and a friendly universe that will instantly answer their pleas for success. When I use visualization, I take the time to go step-by-step from making the call to a potential client to walking into the client's office, sitting down across from the person, and having a conversation that ends with a yes. I then frame a mental picture of the contract being signed.

There are times when your focused visualization can be rudely disrupted by distractions. We all encounter distractions, some that we engender and some that we endure. It's a knock on our office door interrupting us from the finishing touches we're putting on a million-dollar proposal. It's our incessant tether to our smartphone, checking the likes that make us feel good about our last post. It's taking the dog to the groomer's while canceling that initial meeting with a prospect. Be aware of distractions, prioritize what is most important, and stay focused on visualizing the steps it takes to achieve your intended outcome.

The ability to stay focused is a product of the mental discipline you acquire through time, practice, and the ability to prioritize. Willpower is a form of mental discipline that you can use to stay focused. Habit and routine is established and followed from your mind's ability to stay focused on those activities that are beneficial to your personal growth.

You can't allow distractions to block, detour, or derail your path to success. Harsh as it may be, some of these distractions are people. Use tact, be polite, but remember, you either increase the thrust forward or decrease the drag that holds you back. Take a good, hard look at the people you associate with.

You may have heard that you are the sum total of the five people you hang out with the most. Listen to what they have to say and how they say it. Are they blaming others for their circumstance? Are they unwilling to do what it takes to become more? Are they unhappy with their situation but unwilling to do anything to change it? Are they living in the past? Are their greatest victories behind them? Or are they looking for the next challenge? How have they held you back in the past?

Establish your core values, as they are the key to prioritization. What you prioritize, you do. Distractions disguise stagnation; they blur your focus. They come in different forms, shapes, and sizes: social media, people, and the prolonged pursuit of activities that are nothing more than an excuse for not starting.

No matter what, stay true to your core values—and this is a tough one because it might mean you have to distance yourself from some of your friends and acquaintances. Positive influencers and like-minded people share, collaborate, and grow together. Success is a serious business, and those who aren't there to support you will make your life harder. Sure, fun is a part of the game, but prolonged absence from the field of play is nothing more than stagnation.

Speaking of friends and acquaintances, be careful from whom you solicit advice. When you seek the opinion or the counsel of another, it often appears in one of three forms: the *well-intended*, the *ignorant*, or the *malicious*.

Ask yourself:

- However well-intended, does the advice fit with my core values?
- Does this person have the earned credibility to offer this advice?
- Does this person have a hidden agenda with a negative orientation behind the advice?

You can assess the size of people's dreams by the nature and size of the problems that bring them down. And it's not very difficult to ascertain the mental makeup that drives people's motivation; it's found in the nature and size of the problems they solve. If the biggest challenge of their day is reorganizing a file cabinet, it's a safe bet that their level of pay will be commensurate with their level of problem solving. The bigger the problems you can solve, the more value you become to yourself and to the people you work for or with. Solve big problems; cash big checks. It's important to attempt to solve the problem, to think you can, and to try. That's the mental makeup you need to separate yourself from the average. The average are those who push the default button on personal responsibility and blame others for their circumstance, condition, or bad luck.

24/7

Just one weekend. That's all I wanted. For 10 years, I never had a weekend. I could never stay under the sheets, head on the pillow, and open my eyes to nothing. I didn't need an alarm clock. I was up and ready to roll by 5 a.m. I met with clients over breakfast, lunch, and dinner. My fire burned 24/7. It's tempting to choose comfort and slip off the path for a short while. But I know this from experience: It's a bitch to get back on. Once you fall into bad habits, it takes a lot of effort and a lot of willpower to construct new ones.

When I first understood that success was a process and not a destination, I dove into the joy of the day-to-day challenge. Weekends, weekdays—they were just days. All the same to me. I was undeterred and focused, committed to living the sacrifice to achieve the result. I would wake up at 3 a.m. and make calls from the West Coast to London and New York from the darkness of my living room. This was literally clockwork for me. Seven days a week, my internal alarm clock would wake me up to put the week's negotiations in play.

For me, the fun was in the process of pursuit. I was always tinkering with the process, encountering setbacks that I would learn from. Maybe I would veer a little off course, but then I'd get back in the fast lane, headed straight for my goal, because the things we do today to make an impact in our lives are often soon forgotten tomorrow.

Life Outside Your Comfort Zone

Study the successful. They live the habits that unsuccessful people are unwilling to adopt. The successful move outside their comfort zone, accept the pain of change, and treat self-improvement as an obligation. It may be uncomfortable to start something new. But the future regret of neglecting to do those things that could've improved your station in life is a bitter pill to swallow. Regret can be one of the strongest motivators available for your use. Visualize future regret. Regret is an emotional word. It's the one word I know of that if you play it forward, you can feel the hairs on your arm stand up, and you may even choke up. But you can avoid it by making the commitment to yourself to start to do those things that may be a bit uncomfortable at first. Marry yourself to your goal. Build a life today that eliminates regret tomorrow. Put in the time, extend the effort, and when you need a kick in the behind, remember regret. What you think and what you do in the moment, hours, days, or decades will determine whether your life is enriched or impoverished.

Think of it this way: You're hanging out in the middle with the average, and it's not bad at first. There's a lot of company, and everybody more or less shares the same economic profile. People's health may be robust or perhaps good, and they have their entire life in front of them. What a gift! The dream house, the dream spouse, the dream kids, the dream life. Then, there are the few, those who are doing the uncomfortable. They're selective in whom they choose to hang out with. They're serious about their career. They're reading, learning, and associating with people who have big aspirations and are willing to put in the hours to make them real. Both sets of choices look pretty similar at first, and then there's a marked departure. Discomfort sets in for the average; they don't have the finances. They're working paycheck to paycheck. They haven't taken care of their health—and not only does it show physically, but it's reflected in their lack of mental energy.

For some, relationships disintegrate. Lack of drive isn't attractive. The only thing it attracts is money issues, creditors. You once promised each other the dream, but you weren't willing to push the envelope to do what success demanded, and now that dream is tattered and torn. You become angry and frustrated. You point your finger at the successful because either they inherited an unfair advantage, or they were just "lucky."

Deep down, you know that the only person at fault here is you. Once you own and internalize that, what you need is a new definition of comfort. You have to change your thinking about what the comfort zone is, and maybe, just maybe, delay some of your immediate gratifications until you make a way to become successful. But here's the catch: You don't negotiate with success. You have to keep improving, being uncomfortable, failing, learning, and growing by embracing the word that most people fear—change.

No Plan B

There are two commonalities shared by every top producer that I've trained: These people had nothing to lose when they walked in the door. Their bank accounts were under $1,000, and they had no Plan B. It was "make or break." They hustled, dialed, and got in cars, planes, and trains to make things happen. They worked around the country and around the clock. They made it happen for themselves.

A predictable occurrence happened on the way to big money: Once their bank account approximated seven figures, it all changed. These once aggressive warriors put up a moat of safety around their holdings and became satisfied with the status quo they created. They were living literally and figuratively in a place where they never thought they'd inhabit.

Their suits are better, their gait is more assured, and their cars are definitely more expensive. They go where they want, and they don't need to keep doing the nitty-gritty work or learn something new to bring failure (and rejection) up close and personal again.

Training for Success

Your health, relationships, and career need to be nurtured—and that includes the subtle changes that come from the habits you consistently adopt as your lifestyle. When I'm in the gym, I push myself every day for just a little more.

There's probably no better metaphor for failure than those challenges, disappointments, and endorphin highs that come from attempting, failing, and succeeding in the iron war. When I was a skinny kid, I would watch my brother work out religiously with a zeal that I didn't find in any of my activities. I would watch him lift on occasion, and one day, as I was drinking a beer, sitting on the steps to our basement, he asked me if I'd like to try it. I remember putting the beer down by the bench press and trying to lift the 45-pound bar—that's the weight of a lifting bar without any weights on it. The best I could describe it would be, my arms felt like spaghetti trying to control and lift something that was a struggle in futility. He put the bar back on the rack, and said, "Come on, you're not that weak!" I picked my beer back up and went back to my spot on the stairs. But I went back the next day. This time, without a beer. And as humiliating as it was, I started to work with that 45-pound bar, just trying to get my form right. Now this is context for "failing more!"

Breakthroughs to success are first formed from a place of humility. Arrogance forecloses possibility, but humility opens the door to opportunity. The willingness to admit you're wrong or you've failed gives you the power to start over, armed with the experience it takes to successfully accomplish your end. You need your allies and those that support your quest to point out your blind spots and to serve as a source of feedback. My brother was my champion when it came to lifting weights. I watched him, learned from him, and then tried to be him. I was on a quest, and I wasn't going to be derailed or distracted.

Street Smarts and Book Smarts

Learning is the vanguard on your road to success. The lowest yield of learning can provide entertainment and information. Learning can open the gates of inquiry and provide knowledge that is everything from useful to humorous or inspiring and irrelevant.

Let's slice learning into two sections: street smarts and book smarts. Street smarts are a form of situational awareness, a product of our conditioning, experience, and intuition. Street smarts are the vestige of our survival instinct—they attune our emotional bandwidth with the environment.

Street smarts are the product of instinct and good judgment. Book smarts are the product of edification, reflection, and imagination.

Choosing which is "best," street smarts or book smarts, is a binary question that does not lend itself to an objective answer. We need both to survive. We need to use both to move through life in a productive and successful fashion. Street smarts are an "in the trenches" granular form of teaching where good judgment, speed, and the ability to read people swiftly and accurately are essential to survival.

Both Warren Buffett and Mark Cuban cite reading as one of the essential keys to success. In a 2013 article in the *Omaha World-Herald*, Todd Combs (former hedge fund manager and current investment manager at Berkshire Hathaway) recalled the first time he saw Buffett in person. During a lecture with 165 students in a Columbia

University investing class, Combs's classmate asked Buffett how he could best prepare for a career in investing. After thinking for a few moments, Buffett reached for a stack of trade publications, reports, and other documents he had with him. "Read 500 pages like this every day. That's how knowledge works. It builds up, like compound interest. All of you can do it, but I guarantee not many of you will do it." Mark Cuban is also known as a voracious reader. In his online journal, *Blog Maverick,* he posted in May 2004, "Everything I read was public. Anyone could buy the same books and magazines. The same information was available to anyone who wanted it. Turns out most people didn't want it. . . . Of course my wife hates that I read more than 3 hours almost every day, but it gives me a level of comfort and confidence in my businesses."

No matter what you read in a book, you're still one degree of separation away from the experience. On your road to success, you're going to need to combine both street smarts and, to a degree, book smarts.

Experience is a valuable teacher if you're willing and able to learn from the lesson. But some of the lessons you learn from a book can prevent you from making those mistakes on the street that delay or detour your journey on your road forward.

Success leaves clues. While you can't copy and paste someone else's blueprint for success and call it your own, you can learn what worked and what didn't work for those who are successful. You accomplish this by talking with them and observing their actions.

Look around you—find those people who are "killing it" in your industry, profession, or arena. What traits can you emulate? What skills do you need to learn? You can learn from them.

One of the fastest ways to learn from those who are successful is to ask questions. Listen all the way through for the key points and answers. Don't interrupt or interject—let them talk to you before you begin to talk with them. Nothing turns off a seasoned professional like a question from a rookie that the novice answers before the professional can finish. Continually refining your listening skills is a form of improvement you need to embark upon if you're going to create those lifestyle options you visualize.

The Fine Print of Success

Your success will be subject to the limits of your continual improvement. Never stop; always learn; always grow. Your edge will drive you forward. Nothing in life worthy of merit or the notoriety of achievement can be given to you. You must earn it. Earning it is a day-by-day proposition. You'll be faced with competing challenges from overwhelming responsibilities compressed into 24 hours. Your future will be determined by the nature of your priorities. What you do today will influence the quality of your life tomorrow.

Have you ever read the fine print of success? You know, the stuff they don't show you when you think you've arrived? When you think you've arrived, read the warning label attached to success. Success is a destination, a journey, not a place of rest. If you stay at rest in the latter stage, you'll begin to regress. Each milestone you accomplish will bring you closer to the next level of uncertainty. You'll meet the devil at that next level, and the lure of complacency will tempt you toward comfort. You'll want to rest, relax, as you promise yourself you'll get back on the road tomorrow.

We all struggle with feelings of loss and inadequacy. Both fall under the umbrella of uncertainty. To be uncertain is to be human. People don't want to fail at the risk of impairing their image of success. Yes, there will be a devil at the next level, and it will present challenges for you to face and overcome. The next level demands mastery. And mastery is the product of process, failure, and refinement—and all those hours spent in its pursuit. Mastery is next level achievement—and success will always demand your answer to the question, "What's next?"

Framing Failure

1. **Stay focused.**
   You'll be faced with a lot of distractions—shiny objects that look like a great deal or a wonderful opportunity. You can't be all things to all people, and you can't be great at all things. Focus your intention on one big goal. Those who try to become a jack-of-all-trades will master none.

2. **Narrow your options.**

   Succeeding in something new takes time, perseverance, and perspiration. There will always be something new on the horizon. Too many options become one major distraction—stay focused on the one thing that you can master.

3. **Learn to apply the saying, "How do you eat an elephant? One bite at a time!"**

   Master one thing at a time. Do it, own it, and then move on to the next thing you need to learn. Get your priorities straight. What's the most important thing you need to try? If you fail, try again, armed with the knowledge of your recent failure.

4. **It's okay to doubt—but it's imperative to move through it.**

   The only way you can move through doubt is to do something. You may fail, but if you keep trying and you have the talent, you'll accomplish what you need to do.

5. **Own your clock.**

   Be accountable to the time you have—24 hours each day—and don't waste the hours or days in procrastination.

6. **Visualize, visualize, visualize.**

   Every day, picture the big goal. Feel it to your core. Now create those small steps (subgoals) that incrementally move you forward on your road to success.

CHAPTER 8

Embrace Risk

*Failure, when it comes to future risk-taking,
is a gift. Successful risk-takers are often
motivated by failure—it's what tells them that
they aren't done preparing yet. It's inspiration
to work harder, to train better, and to learn
more. They understand that mistakes have
the potential to offer them as much, if not
more, than success in the way of both data and
experience. They don't take failure as a sign to
stop and set their sights on something new.*

—**KAYT SUKEL,** *THE ART OF RISK*

Every time you make a choice in life, you're taking a
risk, and your life is a series of the choices you have
made. Along the way, you may have learned that a non-
choice is also a choice. And depending on the situation,
sometimes nonchoices are your best bet. There is a time to
push forward and a time to pull back. A time for action and
a time for inaction. Intentional inaction is a strategy, not a
withdrawal from the field of play. "Comfortable inaction" is
a form of surrender. It's when you perceive a benefit from

action, but you decide the work involved to realize the gain isn't worth the pain.

When you assess the pain-gain game, know that to risk blindly is foolish. Be logical. Go through the progression of emotions that you associate with the chance you're about to take, and then with pen to paper, write down the logic of how you would do what you need to do to succeed.

Taking intelligent risk is a skill. Use the past to inform the present and positively influence the future. If you're met with failure, conduct a postmortem. Discover what went wrong, and find the failure point(s) that caused the setback. If you're met with success, over time, you will learn to master both: the prospective and the postmortem of success or failure. In order to risk intelligently, you need to:

- BE CLEAR—what is the worst thing that can happen if you fail?
- BE REAL—can you accept it?
- BE PRACTICAL—is there a smaller risk you can take that will provide the momentum and experience you will need to take those bigger chances?
- BE OBJECTIVE—is the greater pain of failure emotional or financial?
- BE PREPARED—do you have what it takes to pursue the risk now? If not, when? Make a commitment to a timeline, do what it takes to prepare, get in position, and go forward.
- BE AWARE—as you're moving through the process, taking risks, and doing what needs to happen to win,

conduct a "process audit." What is effective, and what can be improved upon? Adapt and apply on the fly.

- BE REFLECTIVE—start a success journal and stay with it. Keep up-to-date notes that you can revisit for reference and direction. This is where you can write what worked and what didn't work for you during the course of the day. It's important to stay focused on the *day*. Each day, you can learn from what happened the previous day if it's written down in a straightforward manner. No excuse, no bias—just straight-up facts. You'll find that what you learn every day will impact the week, the week the month, the month the year, and in time, it will make your career.

Assessments and Assumptions

Throughout this book, I've encouraged you to cultivate those allies and advocates who can help you see the blind spots, develop the strategies, and roll out the tactics you need to succeed. Now let's look at the power of gathering those allies in one room to help you anticipate the negative things that could happen by looking back and reviewing failures that happened with similar opportunities. Forensic evaluation of a failed attempt involves a process of review, second-guessing, and the 20/20 vision of hindsight.

The lessons of failure will teach you to make more intelligent assessments and more accurate assumptions for the future. The key to group participation when it comes to learning from failure is to lose the need for blame. Teamwork means it's all for one and one for all in trying to find a way that will benefit each and every team member now and in the future. We develop strategies and tactics in a prospective forum. We gather in the conference room, a place where people aren't afraid to express their opinions—those who have the experience and foresight to offer constructive solutions before the problem arises. We spend time identifying the problem. We assess the worst case, and we come to an agreement, a consensus, and then we strategize.

We ask, "What have we put in play before when we encountered this type of risk? Was it successful, or did it flop? Why did it succeed? Can we emulate the process we used to succeed? Why did it fail? What do we have to avoid? What do we have to add? What do we have to do differently? Is it worth chasing again?"

There's a consensus; we agree it's worth the risk. Now it's time to memorialize our strategy in writing with the tactics we'll use to aggressively go after our desired result. What a departure this style is from my early days in business when I just invented on the fly! This type of behavior taught me an important lesson: At all times, endeavor to know. Don't hazard to guess. Preparation and planning can mitigate the effects of potential failure.

Worst Case Versus Best Case

When I first started my company, I wrongly thought I had to be right, right now. I wanted to look invaluable and perfect. I thought power and respect came from having the right answer at the moment, without taking time to do research or question the weakness in my thinking.

Over time, I wound up losing money because I had to backtrack from my mistakes, and I lost a little bit of credibility with my team as well.

I eventually realized that if I kept making every decision, the people in my company would stop critically thinking. They would just wait for orders and walk around on autopilot, while I wore myself out. I didn't want that. So I crafted a model for decision making that has proved to be invaluable to me and the members of our firm.

The model consists of determining the worst-case and best-case results of a situation and then asking questions. It's not filled with answers. I ask the questions, and the team and I come up with the answers.

WORST CASE	BEST CASE
Play the negative forward. What happens if your worst-case scenario becomes a reality? Before you risk, know your downside.	What's the upside? What is the best-case scenario that you could realize from taking this risk?
What are the financial costs of the risk? Try to make this number finite—best guesses are usually more expensive.	What are the financial rewards of the risk? Whatever estimate you come up with, lower it by 20 percent (the law of managing expectations).
What are the reputational costs involved in the risk?	What is your strategy, and what are the tactics you'll use to achieve it? Every risk is different—take your time and craft a design specific to the risk.

(continued on next page)

WORST CASE	BEST CASE
After quantifying the financial costs and qualifying the potential reputational damage, is the risk worth taking?	Write down the actions you took to mitigate the collateral damage of a worst-case scenario. Not every situation will be the same, but you'll find similarities in each case if you follow with this formula.

Failure taught me that I better well know my worst case before I even start to think about my best case. Failure also taught me that if the company was held captive to my ideas, we would soon be waving the white flag of surrender, because we'd be limited to my options and opinions. In the end, I suppressed my ego and called in people who were much brighter than I am, and together, we created a synthesis of thought and ideas that became our way.

Best- and worst-case outcomes are the most important scenarios to weigh when you're at the crossroads of a decision in life. Every one of your choices engenders a consequence. Each choice is the first step in creating your destination. The upside is easier to create than the downside is to repair. You have to know your downside before you take that first step.

This form of outcome assessment isn't confined to the domain of business. It's a proactive philosophy for a better life. Whether it's marriage, social responsibility, or financial planning, you have to be able to play it forward. Playing it forward means you have to take the time to identify your worst-case and best-case scenarios. Once you've identified these scenarios, always manage your downside *first*.

Once you learn your downside, you can identify the people, tools, strategy, and tactics needed to accomplish the goal. Next you have to have a contingency plan that you can summon to the rescue if things start to flame before the crash-and-burn. A contingency plan addresses the potential fallout from a worst-case event *before* the event occurs. Think of it as a form of planned preparation prior to panicked response.

Constructive Failure

Those who need success like the air they breathe treat setbacks as constructive failure. Constructive failure leaves clues and tools you can use to forge success. The insatiable need to make it, to live your dream, must be far greater than the nuisance of fear. That's right; fear is a nuisance when your sole focus is to improve. Failure is simply a small price you must pay to satisfy the burning desire of what you must have. You gotta be hungry!

The Big Mistakes

Maybe you've been fired, came up short on a promotion, or failed in a relationship. Now you're searching for what went wrong. You ask yourself what happened and try to figure out what to do next. You know you have to do something, but you don't know what it is.

From the ashes of failure, you can make one of two choices: Go all in, no retreat, no surrender, and do everything it takes to succeed in your chosen field of endeavor. The other option is to dabble a little bit in a job, and if it doesn't work out, you can revert to Plan B. The problem with Plan B is it soon becomes your Plan A because you haven't committed to *one* way forward. This doesn't mean you stick with a bad position. Maybe you have to change the backdrop, find a new environment, sell a new product, or change a personal relationship. What it means is you have to know what you want before you enter the arena to earn it.

Refer back to the worst-case and best-case scenario table. What happens if your worst-case scenario becomes a reality? What is the best-case scenario that you could realize from taking this risk? Rationally decide—is it worth it? Are you emotionally invested in the outcome? How much pain are you willing to endure to make your dreams a reality? Now commit! Commitment demands that you make a decision and expend every ounce of energy, expand upon every possibility, and take the cuts and bruises that failure delivers. Don't quit. Stay the course. You will triumph from the travails if you accept failure as a nonnegotiable part of success.

You're going to have setbacks. You're going to be defeated, but if you truly commit and do everything it takes to make it happen for yourself, you'll make it happen. You will win if you persevere.

Success wasn't handed to one of the top salespeople in the commercial insurance industry. Rob W. had to fight, scratch, and claw not only to gain a foothold in the industry, but to stay in it when, against all odds, it looked like he wouldn't make it. His story is one of commitment, resolve, and resilience—the three traits you have to manifest every day if you're going to make your way forward through risk.

Failure weakens the knees of those who won't commit, who don't have the resolve to accept the pain to earn the gain. If you're not resilient, you're going to quit. You're going to bail out with your Plan B (if you have one, that is) before you fight through to break through.

Rob looked into the abyss, and from disappointment and failure, his story is one of desire, failure, possibility, and achievement.

Rob is the eldest of three brothers, bred and raised in Palos Verdes Estates, an affluent area in Southern California. His father, a highly esteemed criminal defense attorney, started his own firm in 1967. The practice of law coursed through the family bloodline; future expectations were made clear during early childhood. Rob and his brother Eddie both attended law school during the same period of time. Eddie excelled; Rob struggled as he spent two years trying to grasp the nuances of contracts and the arcane verbiage of the law before he looked in the mirror. Rob then made the call to his family and opened with, "This isn't my *why*. This stuff just isn't for me." In a family of high achievers, much is expected in order to grow the family legacy.

If Rob was going to contribute to the family's hierarchy of success, it was time for him to begin. He didn't have time to find his *why*; he had to get out there and make his way.

Eddie graduated from law school and would go on to start his own practice as a criminal attorney. John, the youngest brother, graduated from Cal Berkeley, was drafted by the Philadelphia Eagles, and spent nine years as a starting offensive lineman for both Philadelphia and Kansas City. With this context, you can imagine the Olympian standard of expectations and the accompanying pressure of being the eldest in a family of high achievers.

At the age of 26 and with bills to pay, Rob was open to options. He interviewed and was offered a job by a Fortune 500 company in the financial services industry at a starting base of $60,000. Small success can open big doors of opportunity, and after his first year with the company, Rob was offered a bigger territory in New York.

However, as a young, new player in New York, Rob was unknown and disconnected from the power brokers who leveraged favors to make the real deals. New territory development requires an investment in time and capital. Rob's employer was unwilling to extend either, and within the year, the company shuttered its New York office.

Regardless of the reason, Rob failed. When you're at the crossroads of a decision, you have two sources of discernment at your disposal, the head and the gut. You have to use reason and intuition. When they're in concert, you have your direction. Rob was at the crossroads of decision. He believed his next career move had to break the pattern of the familiar; it had to be something different, a change. Change makes you uncomfortable; Rob was willing to be uncomfortable. He knew to his core that if he chose the familiar, he'd be back on the street with that résumé within a year.

At this point in his career, I had known Rob for about six months. We had been introduced by a mutual friend, and he started inviting me for a coffee in exchange for mentorship. During one of our meetings, he asked, "Could I interview with your company?" Now, in my decades of ownership, I have tried to disprove the well-worn adage that you should never hire friends or family. I had hired a few friends in my day, and they all flamed out in mutual disappointment and a level of frustration that, for all intents and purposes, ended the friendship. I didn't want to hire Rob because I valued his friendship and considered the past to be prologue.

He sat across the table from me and began, "Look, it's usually money that comes between friends. Take the money out of it. I'll do this for free. If I don't justify myself in two quarters, you don't have to fire me. I'll just walk away."

No one ever tried that approach! And it wasn't the potential savings in his offer. I took a few days to think it over, talked with management, and called him back. "Okay, we're going to hire you. We'll pay you what we pay all intern producers, but I'm not going to fire you—our sales manager will."

The regeneration of spirit in the wake of adversity is a reflection of one's resolve and resilience. Despite his failures early in his career, Rob exuded the confidence of someone who could and would succeed. He needed to become a success, needed it like the air he breathed. There was no Plan B. There was no surrender. There was only success, no matter the emotional cost.

Rob had dreams behind his fears. If he could overcome his fears, he would live his dreams. He was determined not to let his dreams perish with him. A new career gave him a chance to start over and build a life of his dreams that included a wife, kids, and financial freedom. Success doesn't escape those who demand it as a way of life and are willing and able to do those things that make it their lived reality. Was he afraid of failure? Hell no! He had already failed. He had nothing to lose, and those are always the most dangerous people in the world.

The long, often winding road from the birth of a dream to its execution as successful reality is accompanied by challenge, adversity, failure, and often ridicule. Rob's road to success wasn't only challenging and winding; it was populated for the first six months by obstacles that I didn't think he could surmount.

For six months, I searched for anything—a phrase, an appointment, something that would give me a glimmer of hope. "Was hiring Rob the right decision?" One particular day, Rob invited me into his office to listen to his calls. I had blocked off an hour of my time to assess his progress. I didn't even make it to the second call. On his first call, he pronounced the name of our company "Wood-ridge" instead of "Wood-itch." Flush with embarrassment over the faux pas, he stumbled through the most awkward call I've ever heard in my life, and that includes a long, undistinguished list of my own. He recalls to this day his deep embarrassment when he saw the disappointment and resignation on my face. I was halfway out the door when I heard him say, "I'll get it." I walked down to our CFO's office and said, "We made a mistake."

When things aren't working, I first look at the organization and then the person. I ask myself, "What is it we could be doing differently to position him for the best chance of success?"

"Rob, I want you to shadow me on a call. Observe, and afterward, tell me what you learned." This was a scenario we would revisit time and time again. From listening, he learned. He started to make progress with his calls. What he lacked in knowledge, he made up in effort. He was deficient in the nuances of the industry, but he made a pact with himself to outwork this obstacle. On a normal day, he knocked down 200 calls—about 50 more than the prescribed company level for success!

His calls started to generate appointments, and I would accompany him to the prospect's office. He would listen, and I would engage with his prospects. I gradually brought Rob into the conversation, and his confidence grew with each appointment.

Calculated risk generates consistent reward when you're in a position to win. Positioning to win is a process. You adjust as you go, audit your progress, change where necessary, and make agility your friend.

Indelibly burned into my business memory banks is the visual of Rob and me waiting in the conference room for his first proposal. Rob was perfectly coiffed and sported a bespoke suit, red tie cinched for success. But his external demeanor belied his internal turmoil. Nervously tapping his fingers on the hardcover proposal, he asked, "What mistakes will we make today?"

I said, "Why are you asking me that?"

"Well, my former employer said, 'You can't make any mistakes. Do *not* make a mistake.'" His former company demanded perfection, rather than embracing a process that would lead to improvement through mistakes.

I laughed and said, "Are you serious?" And then I made the statement that 16 years later Rob would remember as his breakthrough moment, "We're going to make them all, but it's not going to matter!"

When Rob heard that statement, abundant relief was evident in his countenance. He sat back in the chair and smiled. During the appointment, Rob was relaxed, more willing to contribute to the conversation. He stayed within his lane—a much more confident person. People feed from and feel your confidence. People want to partner with confident people who are competent. Master both, and they'll call you "big time!" See, when you don't fear failure, you're free to perform at your very best. Heck, you might fall; you might fail—so what? Earn your takeaways, practice, and get back out there.

Rob embraced risk because he had no other choice. No matter what business he entered, he had to go "all in" and make it. Now he could keep trying other businesses, but at a certain point, Rob had to own his success. For him, there was no Plan B. This was all or nothing.

How do you respond to challenge? Are you resilient? How bad do you want it? Because at the end of the business day, it comes down to desire, need, must-have. It comes down to that last push, the one that tests your nerves and your resolve. How you respond to the day-to-day challenges in life will dictate your capacity to learn from failure. Will you have a growth mindset or a fixed mindset? The former, essential to navigate the uncertainty of life; the latter, better left to the theorists in classrooms.

The arousal of your nervous system decreases as your exposure to the familiar increases. Remember, your genetic programming is hardwired for survival. Rob faced his fears every day, but he kept his dreams near, dear, and present. Because to live those dreams, he had to do what he feared. He had to take risks; he had to get up from each bruising failure, each dent to the ego, each embarrassment, minute after minute, hour after hour, days and months at a time. Most would've "rung the bell" and just quit. You let failure win when you quit.

After six months of habituation to the uncertainty of the new, he didn't fear making the calls or going on appointments on his own. He had it down! He knew the conditions that success demanded, and he exceeded them!

Motivational speaker Les Brown shares a powerful perspective about the failure to act upon your dreams:

Imagine, if you will, being on your death bed. And standing around your bed are the ghosts of the ideas, the dreams, the abilities, the talents given to you by life.

And that you for whatever reason, you never acted on those ideas, you never pursued that dream, you never used those talents, we never saw your leadership, you never used your voice, you never wrote that book.

And there they are standing around your bed looking at you with large angry eyes saying we came to you, and only you could have given us life! Now we must die with you forever.

The question is—if you die today, what ideas, what dreams, what abilities, what talents, what gifts, would die with you?

If you're going to live the dream, you've got to make a down payment on it every day. You have to grind out the small wins every hour by adopting the habits that unsuccessful people won't. Establishing realistic goals and working every day to make them a reality is crucial to your success. It's intimidating to think you have to come up with a perfect methodology or plan of action. You don't need a formal plan of action. You just need an outline that you can follow with action steps geared for results.

You either embrace risk as a way forward or run from it. There are only two choices. Time to have a "get-tough" talk with yourself—it's time to kick your own derriere! Nothing can happen unless you put yourself in play and take a risk. There's no perfect time, no magic formula. It's you and your willingness to either do or don't.

Framing Failure

1. Remember to approach risk intelligently.
   Start out with small steps that lean into your uncertainty and discomfort. Uncertainty and discomfort are

growth indicators; while your brain may urge you to resist, limited exposure will habituate you to risk.

2. **Start falling in love with the question, "How?"**
   First know your downside. Then to create upside, ask, "How will I do this?" Study the risk and think of ways to capitalize on its opportunity. Take on the smallest challenge and track your progress until you've accomplished your big goal.

3. **You're in great company—even the most successful entrepreneurs take calculated risks, not wild gambles.**
   A calculated risk weighs worst-case and best-case scenarios. Life is a series of trade-offs. Know what you're willing to give up to gain; this is the trade-off of risk and reward.

4. **Make a choice and then follow through with a course of action that you implement with a sense of urgency.**
   Risk can propel you forward from a fear of failure, but I am not advising you to charge headlong into taking risks. Think first, and then do.

5. **The way over fear is through it.**
   Expose yourself to what you fear. Continual exposure will lessen the severity of the fear. You'll get used to it— at first, it may be a rude and often unwelcome visitor. Over time, it will become your indispensable partner.

6. **Make it a game.**
   You can embrace risk when you make it fun. Risk doesn't have to be a negative term—that's just semantics. Risk is synonymous with opportunity, and opportunity is what you create to live a better life.

CHAPTER 9

Success Is a Process, Not a Destination

You want to hear something shocking?
Eighty-five percent of small businesses in this
country fail within the first two years.
Eighty-five percent! That's a
whole lot of failure.

Warren Buffett said that he would not
invest in any business where the owner
hasn't failed at least twice. I love that truly
wealthy and successful people understand
that failure is part of the process.

—STEVE HARVEY

You now realize the importance of failure as the foundation for improvement. You've learned how to take emotion out of the mix and use a rational approach to assess the *how* and the *why* of your failure. You are now equipped with the tools to analyze, adapt, and implement the lessons to achieve future success. You've accepted the fact that you have to work through pain for ultimate gain. You've also learned how a growth mindset is crucial as you push forward to the next level of achievement. You've done your homework. You've established your goals. Your goals are specific, they are realistic, and they are time-sensitive. You're well on your way to success.

Now it's time to see true failure in action so you can understand why your hard work will be worth it as long as you continue to fight. We'll take a look at how three of the world's most successful people, leaders in their respective fields, have leveraged their failure into something truly amazing. They may not have had this book in hand, but they applied the same philosophy and extracted failure's lessons in their breakthrough to success.

Steve Harvey and the Kings of Comedy

Steve Harvey learned from doing stand-up comedy that the hardest night on stage isn't your opening night. It's the one where you have to perform after a complete failure.

Steve was a part of the Kings of Comedy tour, with Cedric the Entertainer and Bernie Mac, that kicked off in Charlotte, North Carolina. This turned out to be a particularly tough time for Harvey, because his mother had recently passed and his mind was understandably elsewhere.

The Kings had their own individual set for 30 minutes, but on this particular night Cedric went on for 47, and Bernie followed with an hour set. They both owned the room. Steve didn't. He pulled jokes from his recently aired comedy special that most of the people in the audience had already heard, and he was faced with boos, heckling, and dissatisfaction. His attention was divided between focusing on his material and focusing on the discontent in the audience, and he grew more dissatisfied with his material.

The next day, on the way to the airport, Harvey heard a review on the radio by a Charlotte deejay, who ripped into him. The deejay said, "The other Kings were hot—but Harvey was certainly no King of Comedy." He went on to predict disaster for the tour. On the plane to Kansas City, Harvey started to write new material. When the plane landed, he sequestered himself in his hotel room and wrote even more. He was in flow, lost in creation and revisions, and was on his way to producing a brand-new comedy routine for his 45-minute set.

That night, when Bernie Mac knocked on his door to invite him to dinner, Harvey respectfully declined and went back to work on his material. A person without a burning desire, a passion for his craft, and a belief in himself would probably have shrugged off a bad performance, thought, "I'll get it next time," and gone out to party with his friends. When the demand for success burns indelibly inside you, it consumes you with the need to sate it. Steve Harvey had that desire. He recalls sleeping in his car because he had no money and the pain of his last stage appearance and thought, "I'm not going back. Hell no, I'm not going back." For him, there was only one way forward. He had to get out of his emotional funk, roll up his sleeves, and work on his material. Then he had to get up in front of those lights and do what he did best—bring the real Steve

Harvey to the stage. Just let it flow; let it go; let it roll. Extensive preparation enables top-level performance.

It was showtime.

That night, Harvey felt fear and uncertainty, but he walked up on the stage in Kansas City anyway. He was pulled by the power of his dream, and in his words, he "killed it." From that night forward, over a two-year period, he left the stage with a standing ovation. His take on the experience?

In his book *Act Like a Success, Think Like a Success*, Harvey wrote:

> Our first two nights in Charlotte and Kansas City helped me to begin looking at failure differently. I learned that failure doesn't have to be this life-shattering, I'm-never-going-to-do-this-again experience but is, in fact, an opportunity to gain a valuable learning experience. . . . My failure in Charlotte gave me the right experience that I needed to rip up the stage the next night in Kansas City.

And his thoughts on failure in general?

> Everybody experiences fear on some level. I face fear; I face uncertainty; I face moments where I'm not sure. Look, it happens to everybody. Fear is the biggest cause of failure in this country. It's the fear of failure that causes most people never to begin the journey. Fear freezes people. It really does, before you even start. Here's the way you counter fear. You counter fear with the size of your dreams. You have

to dream so big; you have to want something so incredible; the size of your dreams becomes bigger than all of your fears.

Learning Along the Journey:
How to Flow Forward with Failure

Picture this: It's your first job. Your skills are compatible with the company's and the industry's demands. You're in the right environment, management encourages you to try new things, they guide you, and when you make a mistake, they work through it with you. You learn your own blind spots along the way and are given a decision-making matrix of risk and gain that will help you in the future.

You choose to pursue a career in that industry. You have an understandable fear of the unknown—after all, this is all new—but you're learning by making attempts to improve. You start to think about the financial gain that can come from risk, and you balance this with your fear of failing. You decide you want the financial gain and the lifestyle options. This new life is worth the risk to your self-esteem, pride, and ego.

In the beginning, you have more to gain than lose. Sure, you have to pay rent, live with a roommate, and scrape by making your car payments, but you're in the building stage. What is there to really lose? You're playing outside your comfort zone, and it feels good. Things are happening, and you're climbing up the corporate ladder. You're an "intrapreneur," or someone who acts as an entrepreneur within the organization and treats the enterprise as if it were his or her start-up and responsibility.

People are watching and judging. Those who aren't taking risks are jealous and resentful, but you don't care much about these people because you know that not taking risks could lead to a slow and painful death to your career. This was the same experience that Steve Harvey had, just in the comedy world. He knew that people were watching and that some people in the audience could be rivals in the entertainment business and were silently hoping he'd fail. But what really mattered in the end was that he didn't let his internal voice of uncertainty or the external negative chirpings over the radio or otherwise deter him.

David Neeleman—Out of the Blue

Have you ever invested so heavily in a dream that it seemed to fill you with passion just thinking about it? A dream that consumed your every waking hour? When you're this closely attached to your dream, it becomes you. It consumes reality and funnels your focus into managing its stewardship and cultivating its growth.

David Neeleman had this type of dream. It became his passionate pursuit and the underlying purpose of his identity. He is the founder of JetBlue. His first airline was called Morris Air, which was sold to Southwest Airlines for something in the neighborhood of $130 million. Then he became an employee of Southwest, and he lasted a bit longer than I did in a large bureaucracy—about five months. He was fired. He had been miserable there; he felt as if he were losing his mind, trying to cut through the tape, the regulations, and the limitations. He had a five-year non-compete contract, which meant he couldn't start another airline right away. That seemed like a career killer, or at least an opportunity squasher.

People who are invested in their dream don't quit. They don't give up on their vision. They don't retire into obsolescence. They continue the fight; whether it's in the garage or a corporate boardroom, they start again. They begin anew with the purpose they nurtured in the first place, determined to create something better, but at all times, determined to continue to follow their dream.

Many of us would take the cash payout and call it good! Maybe play the corporate game better, but then we'd be living someone else's dream. Dangerous are those who don't give up on themselves or their dream! You can't pay them off; they're not there to be bought. Their dreams aren't for sale. They're not overcome with misery, dread, or the feeling of sorrow. Rather, they're imbued with the fire and the spirit to prove themselves once again.

David didn't wallow in misery or feel sorry for himself. He started planning for his next airline. He *visualized* (an important part in the process of success) all the details of the start-up. He outlined the values and what he perceived to be the customer experience. He created a description of each job in the airline, right down to training and compensation. In hindsight, he called the noncompete the best thing that ever happened to him, because he was able to plan and apply the lessons of a previous failure to create JetBlue.

David Neeleman stayed true to his core values. He believed so deeply in providing a better customer experience (one of his core values) that, instead of taking the money and retiring, he aligned his core values with what he perceived to be a market need. He was right on—the market would reward a different approach. In fact, JetBlue was one of only a few U.S. airlines that made a profit during the downturn in airline travel following the September 11 attacks.

Are your actions in alignment with your core values? Do you believe in them strongly enough to push through the negative, the rejection, and the pain to bring them to life? Funnel your focus through the lens of your core values. Align your internal core values to serve as your personal mission statement. Think about this: When you work in concert with your true core, there can be no fracture from trying to be something or someone else. It's your voice. It's your authentic person. And when you take a hit like David Neeleman did, your values will give you the balance needed to move steadfastly and intrepidly forward.

J.K. Rowling and Rock Bottom

In a commencement speech at Harvard University in 2008, J.K. Rowling told her listeners:

> What I feared most for myself at your age was not poverty, but failure . . . a mere seven years after my graduation day I had failed on an epic scale. An exceptionally short-lived marriage had imploded, and I was jobless, a lone parent and as poor as it

is possible to be in modern Britain without being homeless. By every usual standard, I was the biggest failure I knew. I had no idea that there was going to be what the press has since represented as a kind of fairytale resolution. I had no idea then how far the tunnel extended, and for a long time, any light at the end of it was a hope rather than a reality. Had I really exceeded in anything else, I might never have found the determination to succeed in the one arena where I believed I truly belonged. I was set free, because my greatest fear had been realized, and I was still alive, and I still had a daughter whom I adored, and I had an old typewriter and a big idea. And so rock bottom became the solid foundation on which I rebuilt my life.

J.K. Rowling is the picture of perseverance. She is the manifestation of creativity for the love of the art. She spent years writing, tearing up, rewriting, and crafting from failure the success she has forged for herself today.

Creativity is a form of flow. Uninterrupted, it can reveal a new layer of transformative thought. But life doesn't exist in a vacuum, and just as Rowling created the idea for Harry Potter, she was pulled away by the devastating loss of her mother. She fell into a deep, profound depression. Her creativity was put on pause, and she shelved her work.

She had to find a way to break the pattern of depression, and she chose to do that by taking a job teaching English for one year in Portugal. Rowling used her physical distance from home to create a mindset that would enable her to realize the goal of having the first Harry Potter book completed when she returned to the U.K. And proving that gaining clarity in your goals is critical to their ultimate realization.

The best intents and strongest convictions often crumble and dissolve when met with the reality that is life. In the words of world-famous pugilistic poet Mike Tyson, "Everyone has a plan until they get punched in the mouth." You're in the ring of life creating, and then *bam!* You encounter a scenario that derails your progress. Will you have the resilience to get back up?

While in Portugal, Rowling began writing again. She fell in love there, and the pursuit of the romantic ideal took her focus from Harry Potter again. She married and gave birth to a baby daughter, whom she would later raise alone.

She returned to the U.K. with no job, a half-finished product in Harry Potter, and a baby to care for. She was living off unemployment benefits, struggling with depression, and doing her very best to raise a child on her own. Her reality was now firmly entrenched in rock-bottom despair.

Despite all of this, she kept the dream of Harry Potter alive by writing in the cafés as her daughter slept beside her. Just as Elizabeth Gilbert did (finding her center in what she loved, as we learned in Chapter 2), Rowling gained comfort and confidence from her writing. Despite the nickel-scraping struggle to make ends meet, she recalls being moderately happy during this period. She was living her ultimate fear, and yet she found that it really wasn't as bad as she imagined. There was nothing to be afraid of now. She was living her worst-case scenario, and her work began to reflect that mindset: nothing to lose; let's play the game to win.

She wrote feverishly and finished the first three chapters of Harry Potter. She sent them off to a publisher, who, without haste, rejected her material. She sent them to another publisher, and another, and another. Her mailbox overflowed with rejection letters, but her resilient spirit pulled her forward. She explained her mindset during this period in this way: "Failure meant a stripping away of the inessential. I stopped pretending to myself that I was anything other than what I was and began to direct all my energy into finishing the only work that mattered to me."

Her self-belief, resilience, and unyielding need to write finally gained the attention of a publisher. As the editor was reading her manuscript, his eight-year-old daughter started flipping through chapters and begged her father to read more. The acceptance of her manuscript came with a caveat. The publisher would publish her novel with the warning that she should probably get a day job because she wouldn't make enough money to survive writing children's books.

It must've been sweet to prove everyone wrong, those doubters who rejected her material. Against all odds, she persevered. She embraced her love of writing, and in spite of the intermittent periods of creative famine, she endured and prevailed.

After *Harry Potter and the Sorcerer's Stone* was published, J.K. Rowling, a jobless, single mother, living off employment benefits, would become one of the most successful bestselling authors in history.

There is no such thing as an overnight success. Perseverance is blood, sweat, and tears. It's getting up close and personal with rejection. The successful get used to it. They accept it as a compass reading that directs them to their goal. Then there's that one big factor that won't go away no matter what it is you intend to excel at. The difference between intent and its realization is intentional practice, the process that yields to improvement by doing the work, putting in the hours, making the adjustments, and moving forward against the odds, the naysayers, and the obstacles that would hold you back.

J.K. Rowling offers us a challenge and a call to action when she says, "It is impossible to live without failing at something unless you live so cautiously that you might as well not have lived at all—in which case, you failed by default." The Harry Potter series has earned over $400 million in book sales; the adaptation from book to big screen has made the series the third-highest-grossing film franchise of all time. Its eight films have grossed more than $8.5 billion worldwide.

Framing Failure

1. **Do not be a victim.**

   Exercise choice. Lose excuses. Be accountable and take ownership of your life. Those best able to adapt, adopt, and collaborate will flourish.

2. **Life serves adversity as a barrier to entry in the pursuit of happiness.**

   Do you have what it takes to turn adversity into an advantage?

3. **Don't measure your self-esteem based on an external event.**

   Your internal worth must be separated from the value that society at large places on the external or material. When you measure yourself by material gain, title, or status, you will rise and fall based on things beyond your span of control.

4. **Look within as you work to create value for people by first becoming of value to yourself.**

   Values reflect your character. Make sure your thought, word, and deed are in alignment.

5. **Enjoy the fruits of your labor while you are engaged in their pursuit.**

   Take time to break away from the madness, the deadlines, the rush to achieve, and the anarchy of unscripted uncertainty that is a part of business—live a full life in balance and harmony.

CHAPTER 10

Maintain a Mindset for Continued Success

When you find yourself in the thickness
of pursuing a goal or dream, stop only
to rest. Momentum builds success.

—SUZY KASSEM, *RISE UP AND SALUTE THE*

SUN: THE WRITINGS OF SUZY KASSEM

Stagnation is the lack of activity, growth, or development. Without activity, there can be no growth; without growth, there can be no development. The first step in achieving growth demands change.

Most of us work up to our definition of success. We reach a certain point in our journey—maybe it's a point we never thought we'd approximate—and then we tend to try to hold on to what we've accumulated. It may be a title, a salary, or a relationship, and we lay off the gas. We quit doing what enabled us to enjoy the life we currently have, and by doing this, we start to stagnate.

Stagnation pulls you back, so you have to work every day to keep improving—whether it's physically, emotionally, or intellectually. Nature doesn't support the static:

Nature, by definition, is dynamic. You evolve and adapt, or you become obsolete. It's often a rude wake-up call for those who think they can sit on success. You can't. Success is always under construction. It's always going to demand you do something to prove that you deserve it.

When the wake-up call comes, there's shock followed by the struggle to get back in the momentum you previously created for yourself. The longer you disengage from productive activity, the harder it's going to be for you to maintain what you currently worked so diligently for. It's just like when you go to the gym for two weeks straight and then decide to take a Sunday off. That Monday becomes harder than ever because you broke the momentum you were building for yourself.

Sweat Isn't Optional

Leasing real estate can be a confusing process, requiring the guidance of professionals. It was 1993, time to move my ideas from my study at home to a physical location to start my company. After I did extensive due diligence, I selected Cynthia T., an aggressive, personable representative, to secure my leasing needs.

She worked hard, kept me in the loop through the entire process, found out what best fit my needs, and then began negotiations to ensure I was getting the best deal. Her work ethic had enabled her to live at the beach, drive a nice car, and work out in an exclusive gym—one of those high-priced, elite places where sweat is optional.

I was happy with my space, and I was starting to fill it with employees. She called me to check in, and then she asked for a meeting to talk about "other business-related issues." The commercial real estate market was soft, and Cynthia's fortune changed with the market. We met and discussed the market, and she asked the question that would alter the future for both of us, "Can you tell me more about your industry?" Her implicit intent was to do a little reconnaissance and explore the possibility of working at The Wooditch Company.

I gave her a 30,000-foot perspective of the industry, including the work ethic and expectations that were non-negotiable for my sales team. When I finished, I asked her about strategy. Had she anticipated the change in the market? And specifically, what kind of actions did she take when the market turned soft?

I expected her to tell me she "turned up" her activity level, but her answer disabused my expectation. She told me she didn't have as much activity, but what she did was go after the higher-end, bigger-commission clients. She had been making 50 to 60 drive-by calls per week, and she cut back to 20 or 25 in more exclusive neighborhoods. She had been sending out 25 e-mails and 20 mailers a week, but she cut back to a dozen in a higher-end market. Instead of making 75 calls each week, her volume shrunk to no more than 30.

Sales is a numbers game, and no matter how you look at it, activity will rule your success. You've got to keep your pipeline full. I thought her failure was a direct result of her cutbacks in the crucial area of activity.

Despite her declining results in real estate, I still thought Cynthia had the DNA to excel in sales. She had that personality that connects with people—honest, forthright—and I thought with the right mentoring, she could be a major player in the industry.

You can't do other people's push-ups for them. You can't consistently motivate or inspire them to a higher level of effort. That's all about the individual. What you can do is provide the environment, or make sure you're in the environment that rewards your activity.

Cynthia came back to me five times in two weeks to talk about the opportunity. She didn't seem desperate, but she did seem hungry. Without clearly defined expectations from management, people will establish their own criteria for accomplishment. I was going to bring crystal clarity to the opportunity I was about to offer Cynthia. I laid out a low base salary with a high commission structure that she was used to, and at first, she balked.

People get used to a certain lifestyle from the compensation they earn, and they fail to look at the fact that if they don't continue to grow and earn more, forces outside their control will change—as will their income. This is why stagnation is so dangerous. You'll face a crossroads of choice. Either you move through stagnation and grow your value to increase your lifestyle options through more income, or you will stop, try to hang on to what you have, and then find out that you have to shrink your lifestyle options to fit your smaller paycheck.

"I can't live on that amount. I need more security than that. Even for a short period of time, it's too little." She was adamant, but I was intractable. I pushed back from the table, and in a measured tone, I laid out the logic behind what I thought was a universal law: Without risk, there can be no reward. She would have to shrink her lifestyle for the short term in order to expand it exponentially in the long term. My system was proven—if she would follow the rule of activity, she could make it.

Reluctantly, and perhaps because she was out of other options, she took me up on my offer.

The first four weeks were hell for me and her.

She would burst out of my office, tears flowing, panicked. The people she was calling weren't talking to her. She would lose her beach house, and the repo man would take her car in the middle of the night. She was playing out the worst-case scenario, stalled by imagined fear. "Cynthia, right now, your fears are irrational. If you don't follow my rule for activity, then they'll become *rational* reasons for fear. Why? Because you're not doing the work!"

Her past failure was due to stagnation. She became complacent; she stopped engaging in the activity that created her success, the home at the beach, the car, and, yes, the overpriced gym membership. I directed her back to the phone and monitored her progress. I couldn't do the work for her, but I could remain vigilant and present to make sure she did the work.

Cynthia's success was her responsibility. Rationally, I accepted this fact, but emotionally, I rejected this option. I knew she could succeed, but she had to want success for herself more than I wanted it for her. She turned her fear into activity, and she turned up the number of calls and drive-bys exponentially! She was smashing my minimum expectation of 150 calls a day and establishing real contacts.

Her activity began to pay off. She was setting appointments and closing deals! In seven months, she had a bounce of confidence that grew with each paycheck. It was all smiles and fun at The Wooditch Company, right up until her activity began to drop again!

Stagnation sneaks up on all of us, and damn if it didn't creep right up into her office again! Her calls dwindled to 100, then 90, then 80. She took long lunch breaks, her appointment calendar grew thin, and the commission checks dwindled.

I pulled her into my office. I let her know that if her call volume dipped below 150 on any given day, I would terminate her right on the spot. Heart only goes so far until "tough love" is the only option.

Six months later, we were back to the land of milk and honey. All smiles, fat bonus checks, sales nirvana! Cynthia understood the dangers of stagnation, and the feelings of fear and loss were her motivation to do what was required to succeed.

Cynthia kept her call volume high over the years, and in times of sentimentality or appreciation—perhaps both— she would thank me for the tough lesson that enabled her to buy a bigger house and more cars, and if she chose, to start her own gym!

Remember, personal responsibility creates momentum, and momentum's sustained, productive forward motion is a cure for stagnation. Cases like Cynthia's confirm my belief that the biggest predictor of success isn't how smart you are, how talented you are, or how handsome or pretty you are, but rather how willing you are to fail, study your failures, learn from them, and apply that hard-earned knowledge with consistency.

Acknowledging that a change needs to be made is the first step in making a change. When the discomfort of staying the same overrides the assumed pain of change, people change.

Cynthia was motivated to make a change in her life. Perhaps you're at that point where you're motivated to make the change. You've played it forward in your head. You need to strive for something more; you want something better for yourself and perhaps your loved ones. Before you move forward, it may be beneficial to reflect— past experience can shed light on successful and negative patterns. You'll find lessons in both success and failure hiding in plain sight.

You've reflected. Now it's time to ask yourself the questions that only you can answer:

- What is holding me back?
- Am I being honest with myself in my current assessment?
- Is there a common theme in the patterns of my past behavior that I can replicate or eradicate?
- Realistically, where can I set my bar of expectations?

Personal responsibility creates momentum, and momentum is the antithesis of stagnation. You generate momentum when you lose excuses and swing into action. Excuses are a weak person's crutch—you don't need them to move forward. Excuses will make you stagnant, and losing them will give you power. Own this power, and those around you will appreciate your honesty and unwillingness to assign blame to other people, the environment, or current conditions.

Set Up Your Day for Success

A good start to your morning provides the impetus for positive momentum. Momentum is an accumulation of energy. It is the embodiment of accomplishment through forward-thinking vision or action. Momentum builds from the previous day, week, and month. It takes a tremendous amount of effort to achieve true momentum. It takes very little inactivity to lose it.

Start your day with the intent to maximize opportunities and set up tomorrow's thoughts and actions today. Start early, before game time, and get ready to go when the clock strikes "now!"

Here are a few starting points to ensure that each day starts off right:

- UNDERSTAND THE DIFFERENCE BETWEEN WHAT IS *IMPORTANT* AND WHAT IS *URGENT.* Just because things come at you in a rush doesn't mean they're important. Anything that has a great significance or a real value that can have a profound effect on success, well-being, or survival is *important.* Anything that requires immediate action or attention is *urgent.* They're not mutually exclusive. Some things that are important are urgent. However, not all things that are urgent are important.

Here's an example: Let's say you're a manager and you have an open-door policy. You're working through your priorities, performing the functions that are *important* in your job. A coworker rushes in with his "hair on fire" and drops one of his *urgent* problems on your desk. (Often, the reason it's *urgent* is because he didn't treat it as *important* in the first place!) Now, as the manager, you have a choice. Either you can drop what you're doing, putting your client's needs on the back burner, and put out the fire. Or you can coach your coworker on what to do before an opportunity becomes an urgent problem. I think the better option is obvious.

- FOCUS ON CREATIVITY. Imagine yourself in a state of flow. What does your environment look like? Often your environment looks like rush hour in New York City with objects coming at you at warp speed. It's a mental and often physical overload—stress, dead-lines, and those last-minute, urgent requests. You need to find a place to break away, a place where you can strategize the night before about the activities and accomplishments you will achieve the next day. This is a forum where you lose the focus on detail and gain the big picture of vision. For me, I use this forum to cleanse my mind of all the daily problems or issues that forced me to focus on detail while chasing away my creativity. I then retreat to my place of flow and recapture my creativity in a quiet place without phones or people to cloud my vision, a vision I need to keep me focused and clear with my major goal.

Think of the "forest and the trees" analogy. Sometimes, you don't see the forest for the trees. The trees are the detail, and the forest is the big picture you paint from creativity.

- BE FLEXIBLE. Life demands flexibility, as last-minute requests, unexpected events, and other interruptions are an inevitable part of your day. Embrace the fact that change will enter your day at some point. You have to be able to adapt to those people and issues that may interrupt your routine. Adjust, adapt, and get back to the habits that make for a successful day. While you're at it, prioritize your work and start crossing items off your list.

  As you'll recall, for J.K. Rowling flexibility was vital to survival. She found a way to survive by taking her infant child with her as she sat in a café, working away at her writing. By engaging in flexibility, she provided a product that enabled her to thrive.

- ADD UP YOUR SMALL WINS. Find a way to incrementally achieve or win the day even when obstacles try to impede your progress. These small, individual wins will add up to a big victory once you put this into practice.

- EXECUTE. Once you've set up your day in order of importance, start getting things off your list. Execute! Without aggressive action to support them, the best-prepared plans are nothing but wish, hope, and fantasy. Remember Stephen King and his mountain of rejection letters? He kept writing, and writing, and writing. Eventually he got a letter that rejected him but gave him the encouragement he needed to keep going, find the right place for his stories, and ultimately land him a book deal.

Once you execute these steps, you will have planned your day through careful design, effort, resilience, and result. By structuring your day this way, you prepare yourself for the challenges of tomorrow. Do this by learning from previous mistakes and taking the time to learn. Don't settle; feel the restless urge to improve. Life is supported by forward progress. Progress is the product of structured discipline and focused activity.

Framing Failure

1. **Embrace the struggle.**
   There's a high, an endorphin release, that comes from achievement. Often the process that leads to accomplishment brings a greater high than the achievement itself. So enjoy the struggle when you're engaged in the process. And when it's time to pop the cork on the champagne, you can look back with appreciation and perhaps a bit of sadness—this chapter is gone.

   People with a fixed mindset believe that ability is fixed; it's innate. They're the ones who are uncomfortable with challenge. They're accustomed to achievement, but when achievement doesn't follow their formulaic effort,

173

they often quit. They haven't learned to fail, and when the thirteenth proposal is rejected, they often take their toys and go home.

"Frustration is the signal that the breakthrough is coming," writes Steven Kotler in *The Rise of Superman: Decoding the Science of Ultimate Human Performance*. You build muscle from time under tension—the struggle to complete that last rep where you push and push until your strength fails. Ironically, this type of failure yields growth. In the gym, you've got to fail more to improve more!

2. **Set up feedback mechanisms.**

In one of her studies, Carol Dweck measured brain activity as test participants answered questions and received feedback. The brains of the people with the growth mindset lit up when those people learned if their answers were right or wrong—their brains also showed activity when the program went on to explain a wrong answer. Those with a fixed mindset ignored constructive feedback and only focused on whether their answers were right or wrong. Once they found the answer, their interest waned, and for the purpose of the exercise, their neural activity switched off.

Feedback is crucial to refinement, and refinement occurs through learning the lessons of failure. Pay attention to the constructive feedback you get. There's often something of value that you can apply from the messenger or the message—you can then decide whether it's valuable information or something to be dismissed.

3. **Follow your obligation.**

    Stagnation is the renunciation of personal responsibility. You have one life—you get one lap around the track. You have an obligation to live a fully engaged life, not a stagnant existence.

    Stagnation leads to delay, and over time, to decay. When complacency sets in, it's a tough state to overcome. There is no more life-stifling feeling than the powerlessness that accompanies stagnation. Don't renounce your vitality and vibrancy on the couch of comfort.

Afterword

Life is not a success-only a journey. You are
going to get beat up along the way. And
you've got to have the strength of character
to get up and get back in the game.
—PHILLIP C. MCGRAW

How many times have you beaten yourself up, dwelled on the negative, or failed to let go of the past? Developing mental toughness, or the ability to bounce back, will result in your being stronger, faster, better, more determined than ever.

Success is like the stages of a rocket—each level burns off at a certain point and must be replaced by a stronger push to reach an even higher stratosphere. You reach the next level of success when you learn how to respond to failure. Your next level of achievement will be contingent upon your ability to learn the lessons of failure and apply them for growth.

You'll need to adopt a mindset of mental toughness to respond to failure. You'll encounter obstacles, and you'll need to be resilient and resourceful to overcome them. Some of these impediments will test your resolve. Just keep your eye on the goal and take it one step at a time—and know that because of all your hard work throughout this book, you are prepared to recover and shine after any failure that comes your way.

You may have heard a lot about *grit* and how important it is as an enabler for success. It's up to you to develop the grit you need to succeed. Grit is developed from the practice of fundamentals; it's doing the stuff no one wants to do and maintaining the course when others drop off.

Don't be bashful; talk to successful people! It's crucial for you to find friends or allies who are successful, who have gone through some of the tests and challenges (maybe in a different space within business) that you are now facing. Ask them questions, and above all, learn how to use feedback.

Know you will fail again. It's part of reaching the next stratosphere of development. Make a commitment to the integrity of your process, or if it's not working, change it. Be flexible, and don't stay with a system that does not move the needle toward your goal. Blow it up and start over.

Adjust, adjust, adjust. Use a growth mindset; be flexible; don't make failure as personal as those with a fixed mindset. Anything of significance in your life can only be created from the detritus of failure. Understand it comes with bumps and bruises, but it also comes with an enjoyment that accompanies successfully implementing the lessons of failure.

Become your own advocate. Learn to define failure on your terms, not society's. An advocate fights for a cause—make sure you fight for yours. Start viewing your failures as a reflection of your willingness to take a risk. Keep risking intelligently. Reward comes from risk, and nothing can happen without it. It's your personal obligation to make it happen for yourself.

And remember to take a deep breath and summon your reason to think it through. Ask yourself, "Is this something I want? Am I willing to face my fears to get it?" If the answer is yes, find those people who can help you get where you want to be, learn from them, and then take small steps toward what it is that you must have.

Compete with Yourself

Find your conviction, learn what it means to be compelled by something bigger than yourself, and don't accept anything less than your best every day. If you're going to put in only half the effort, you should save yourself the frustration, time, and energy and stay on the sidelines of life as an observer instead of a participant. The depth of your character is revealed through action, and comparing yourself with others is not just a losing proposition, but a waste of time and an invitation for frustration and disappointment. By doing that which others fear they can't, you'll be in elite company. Those who become paralyzed by their fears think they can't and never show up. They aren't your competition.

Greatness is an aspiration, a calling, a striving, a process, and a pursuit that is first guided by improving the self, and then, at its highest level, directed toward sharing, collaborating, and contributing to the welfare of others.

179

Don't concern yourself with burning out. Find your pace and work at it. Sometimes you need to sprint, take a break, begin to sprint again, and then start to jog. The key is, just keep moving forward. As long as you get to the finish line, that's the goal. The purpose of the exercise is to create a better life, not become a slave to the exercise. This philosophy extends to each of our precious reserves: mind, body, spirit, and emotion.

Happiness results from creating a better way of life. French philosopher, author, and journalist Albert Camus had this to say about the search for happiness, "You will never be happy if you continue to search for what happiness consists of. You will never live if you are looking for the meaning of life." When we create the conditions that foster it, happiness appears as a state of overall well-being and personal prosperity. The conditions that foster happiness have their origin in failure. This may sound like pretzel logic, but sustained achievement is the product of intermittent failure.

Happiness begins with accepting who you are for what you are; and it continues with your being comfortable in your own skin and accepting your failures as a rite of passage that success demands. What you are is human, a person with flaws, foibles, insecurities, doubts, and fears. We each have the potential to change, improve, adapt, and evolve. Potential can only become realized when you force yourself from stagnation and take that first step into something new. And that is to step into your fear. When you step into fear, you move closer to your goal. No one can hand you your goal, you have to earn it, and you earn it by moving through fear and embracing the lessons of failure.

Take the First Step

Life, liberty, and the pursuit of happiness are unalienable rights that we each have an obligation to pursue. Happiness comes at a cost, a cost that includes vision, sacrifice, resolve, introspection, and continued improvement.

My hope for you is to find the courage to do the work and take the first step. I want you to begin to create the lifestyle options that many dream of and few live. Choose to live your dreams by making responsible, intelligent choices. I have written this book for those who are determined to create a better way—who take personal responsibility for finding or making their own way in life, business, and relationships. This book is for those prepared to do the internal work to move forward in spite of fear and the constant specter of failure, for the courageous who are willing to earn their success in the crucible of failure. Liberty is freedom, and freedom involves choices and the courage to act upon those choices.

Happiness ensues when you pursue your freedom with self-responsibility, discipline, and courage. If you're going to create a better way of life and enjoy true happiness, you have to seek levels of improvement every day. As you seek better, perhaps more, you're going to encounter setbacks, you're going to have missteps, and you're going to fail. In *Fail More*, I have provided a blueprint to understand the nature of your fear and to use the tools outlined in the book to break through the sting of rejection and the despair of defeat to enjoy the deepest levels of true success.

Index

About the Author

After spending a year at a dead-end job with a foreclosed future, Bill Wooditch "found a way and made a way" from the impoverished backwoods of western Pennsylvania to create a multi-million-dollar company. He is the founder and CEO of The Wooditch Group, a risk-management and corporate insurance firm.

Today, Bill is on a mission to help people improve their lifestyle options. He mentors those who are hungry for success, teaching them skills to harness the lessons of failure to create new opportunities. His approach is a physical, intellectual, spiritual, and emotional journey based on 25 years in-the-trenches, from rough-hewn job sites to highly veneered Fortune 500 boardrooms.